PRINCIPAL

HOW TO TRAIN, RECRUIT, SELECT INDUCT, AND EVALUATE LEADERS FOR AMERICA'S SCHOOLS

Mark E. Anderson

ERIC Clearinghouse on Educational Management
College of Education • University of Oregon
1991

Design: Leeann August

International Standard Book Number: 0-86552-106-9
ERIC/CEM Accession Number: EA 023 124

Printed in the United States of America, 1991
ERIC Clearinghouse on Educational Management
University of Oregon, Eugene, OR 97403

Prior to publication, this manuscript was submitted for critical review and determination of professional competence. The publication has met such standards. The publication was prepared with funding from the Office of Educational Research and Improvement, U.S. Department of Education, under contract no. OERI-R 188062004. The opinions expressed in this report do not necessarily reflect the positions or policies of the Department of Education.

No federal funds were used in the printing of this publication.

The University of Oregon is an equal opportunity, affirmative action institution committed to cultural diversity.

Mission of ERIC
and the Clearinghouse

The Educational Resources Information Center (ERIC) is a national information system operated by the U.S. Department of Education. ERIC serves the educational community by disseminating research results and other resource information that can be used in developing more effective educational programs.

The ERIC Clearinghouse on Educational Management, one of several such units in the system, was established at the University of Oregon in 1966. The Clearinghouse and its companion units process research reports and journal articles for announcement in ERIC's index and abstract bulletins.

Research reports are announced in *Resources in Education (RIE)*, available in many libraries and by subscription from the United States Government Printing Office, Washington, D.C. 20402.

Most of the documents listed in *RIE* can be purchased through the ERIC Document Reproduction Service, operated by Cincinnati Bell Information Systems.

Journal articles are announced in *Current Index to Journals in Education. CIJE* is also available in many libraries and can be ordered from Oryx Press, 4041 North Central Ave., Suite 700, Phoenix, Arizona 85012. Semiannual cumulations can be ordered separately.

Besides processing documents and journal articles, the Clearinghouse prepares bibliographies, literature reviews, monographs, and other interpretive research studies on topics in its educational area.

Clearinghouse
National Advisory Board

CONTENTS

PREFACE

The ERIC Clearinghouse on Educational Management is pleased to add this book to the School Management Digest Series. The goal of the series is to provide concise, readable analyses of both research evidence and practical wisdom on important issues facing today's school leaders. Each Digest points up practical implications of major research findings so that its readers might better grasp and apply knowledge useful for the operation of the schools.

In this Digest, Mark E. Anderson skillfully combines knowledge from both print and practice in a lucid examination of the training, recruitment, selection, induction, and evaluation of America's principals. He summarizes key findings from recent literature on the principalship and also draws from interviews with leading educators and school districts' descriptions of their successful programs. The result is a scholarly yet practical monograph that will be of value to principals and their trainers, recruiters, and supervisors.

Anderson is director of employment services for the Mukilteo School District in Everett, Washington. Anderson received his Ph.D. from the University of Oregon's Division of Educational Policy and Management in 1989. While pursuing his doctoral studies, he served as a graduate research assistant for the Oregon School Study Council and as a research analyst and writer for the ERIC Clearinghouse on Educational Management.

Anderson's ten years of experience as a principal in Washington State give him practical as well as theoretical understanding of the needs and challenges confronting principals. In 1987, he was selected as an Outstanding Regional Director of Principals by the Association of Washington School Principals (AWSP). Anderson has been a presenter at AWSP's Beginning Principal Conference, the Washington and Oregon Association of School Personnel Administrators' joint conference, and the Confederation of Oregon School Administrators conference.

Philip K. Piele
Professor and Director

AUTHOR'S PREFACE

Principals—what they do and who they are—have been of interest to me since early childhood. Being raised in a principal's home exposed me to the principalship at an early age and influenced my own work as a school principal. This volume, therefore, results from living, working, and thinking with those individuals who chose to be principals.

What training is needed to be an effective school leader? Whom do school districts prefer to hire? How are principals introduced to their jobs? What type of feedback on performance do they need and receive? Why do some principals succeed while others fail? Not only have I asked and thought about these questions, all individuals interested in principalships ask them when contemplating this important school leadership position.

My search for answers to those questions led me to enter the doctoral program in the University of Oregon's Division of Educational Policy and Management. My abiding interest in those questions shaped my dissertation topic: the induction experiences of beginning principals. As a graduate teaching fellow for the ERIC Clearinghouse on Educational Management and the Oregon School Study Council, I was given access to a rich collection of research literature about principals, which, together with data obtained through my field research, yielded insights into how training programs and school districts could help individuals become capable school leaders. This School Management Digest provides some answers to the questions that I and many others have raised when reflecting upon life as a school principal.

Material from the chapters on training, recruitment and selection, and induction appeared originally in the ERIC Clearinghouse on Educational Management's book *School Leadership: Handbook for Excellence* (1989) and in two Oregon School Study Council (OSSC) Bulletins, *Hiring Capable Principals: How School Districts Recruit, Groom, and Select the Best Candidates* (May 1988) and *Inducting Principals: How School Districts Help Beginners Succeed* (October 1988). A significant part of the chapter on evaluation was first published in another OSSC Bulletin, *Evaluating Principals: Strategies to Assess and Enhance Their Performance* (May 1989). Practical examples used in the text come largely from anecdotes shared by administrators during interviews conducted for the ERIC and OSSC publications mentioned above.

I wish to thank Stuart C. Smith, director of publications for the ERIC Clearinghouse on Educational Management and editor of the Oregon School Study Council, for his help in planning this work. He provided excellent editorial assistance and has been very supportive of my work as a writer for ERIC and OSSC. In addition, special thanks are due to Dr. Philip K. Piele, director of the ERIC Clearinghouse on Educational Management. As my graduate advisor and dissertation committee chair, I have appreciated Dr. Piele's advocacy of my work.

FOREWORD

Mark Anderson has compiled a book that is both informative and disquieting. He offers us a comprehensive review of current thinking about the preparation, selection, and assessment of school administrators. Such information heretofor has been unavailable under one cover.

The book offers numerous insights concerning contemporary efforts to train, recruit, select, induct, and evaluate the individuals who control our schools. Given that a principal of a moderate-sized school affects the lives of thousands of young people and hundreds of professionals over the span of an administrative career, such insights deserve our careful attention.

What is worrisome about Anderson's book, however, is that it reveals the substantial gaps in our knowledge base about principals. We simply do not know enough about how to develop and sustain good leaders of schools.

Consider the matter of prediction. The ability to predict is the grail sought by many social scientists. Unfortunately, our present knowledge base does not permit us to predict, with reasonable accuracy, the type of principal needed for a particular organizational situation (opening a new school, closing an established school, turning around a school experiencing declining student achievement, leading a school with aging faculty). Nor can we predict accurately what attributes or characteristics of particular principals will contribute to their effectiveness.

Part of the problem, alas, is a curious lack of agreement about what constitutes effective school leadership. Patron satisfaction, teacher satisfaction, loyalty to the superintendent, student achievement, school climate, and mastery of lists of leadership competencies all have been offered as bases for judging a principal's effectiveness. Whether these criteria are interrelated or not is, at this point, sheer speculation.

It follows, of course, that if we are unclear about the criteria for judging a principal's effectiveness and if we are unable to predict what type of principal is best suited to particular situations, we are not going to feel very confident about how we prepare, select, or evaluate principals. Faced with so many uncertainties, we frequently rely on our observations of what principals do. Principal preparation and inservice programs, recruitment and selection criteria, and evaluation categories often are based on analyses of principals' actual behavior. Yet, if we listen carefully to principals, we often hear them complaining that they are unable to spend their time the way they would choose. Many principals feel their talents are underutilized.

Lack of sufficient knowledge, or course, rarely prevents us from taking action. So we go about the business of training, recruiting, selecting, inducting, and evaluating school leaders. What we currently do in these areas is ably described in this unique and useful volume. Still, there remain for the serious reader a host of nagging questions:

- Is what it takes to become a school leader related to what is required to be an effective school leader?
- Are institutions of higher education the best places to offer preservice programs for principals?
- Is it possible that the knowledge most sought by prospective principals is the knowledge least likely to spawn effective or transformational leadership?
- Does the thinking and functioning of principals evolve over time?
- Do the factors that make a particular principal effective change over time?
- Is it safe to surmise that no principal is equipped equally well to deal with every school situation?

Until we can answer questions such as these, those of us involved in the preparation and supervision of school leaders are apt to continue to feel uneasy.

Daniel L. Duke
University of Virginia
Charlottesville, Virginia

INTRODUCTION

The last decade's research on effective schools and the current call for school reform both point to the principal as a key person in the quest to create excellent schools. Virtually all research on effective schools identifies principal leadership as critical for instructional improvement in the classroom and vital to the overall success of a school. A report from the Select Committee on Equal Educational Opportunity of the United States Senate captures the importance of the men and women who occupy the pivotal position of school principal:

> In many ways the school principal is the most important and influential individual in any school.... It is his [her] leadership that sets the tone of the school, the climate for learning, the level of professionalism and morale of teachers, and the degree of concern for what students may or may not become. If a school is a vibrant, innovative, child-centered place; if it has a reputation for excellence; if it has a reputation for excellence in teaching; if students are performing to the best of their ability, one can always point to the principal's leadership as the key to success. (Weldy 1979)

During the 1990s, nearly 60 percent of all current principals in the United States will retire. This decade, therefore, presents a "window of opportunity" for school districts to hire many talented new principals who can lead our nation's schools into the twenty-first century. As a recent publication on principal selection from the U.S. Department of Education suggests:

> We must take this opportunity to fill our schools with dynamic, committed leaders, for they provide the key to effective schools where we will either win or lose the battle for excellence in education.

Unfortunately, the means by which American principals are trained, selected, inducted, and evaluated are often ill-suited to the development and employment of outstanding leaders. School practitioners often voice concern about the preservice

1

training of school principals, contending that university programs do not adequately prepare aspiring administrators for the complexity of the principalship. In addition, several studies and leading educators suggest that school districts may not invest sufficient time, energy, and money to identify, train, select, induct, and evaluate principals.

As troubling as this might sound, an encouraging sign—documented in this School Management Digest—is that many districts are willing to make the necessary investments to groom, hire, and retain the most capable principals. In addition, some universities are improving their principal preparation programs. They are working with school districts to bridge the gap between the theoretical concepts of school administration taught in university classrooms and the practical aspects of the principal's role.

Given the importance of the principalship and the pending turnover of principals, this Digest examines the training, recruitment, selection, induction, and evaluation of America's principals. It summarizes research and leading educators' opinions on these topics and documents strategies that characterize successful programs in the areas of principal training, selection, induction, and evaluation. Practicing and aspiring administrators, school board members, and educators who want to capitalize on the coming "window of opportunity" can use strategies presented in this Digest to assess their principal preparation, recruitment, selection, induction, and evaluation methods.

PRINCIPALS

HOW TO **TRAIN**, RECRUIT, SELECT, INDUCT, AND EVALUATE LEADERS FOR AMERICA'S SCHOOLS

TRAINING PRINCIPALS

$\mathbf{A}$ re outstanding school principals born or made? Most modern authorities, stressing nurture over nature, believe that major competencies of leadership can be learned. Nevertheless, school administrators and trainers of administrators have grappled for some time with identifying effective methods to prepare individuals to be successful principals. Traditional avenues to the principalship, including teaching experience, coursework at a university, a practicum, and even a tour of duty as a vice-principal, have been found less than satisfactory. Practitioners complain the loudest, however, about their graduate training. This chapter describes problems in the preparation of principals, argues for more hands-on training opportunities, and offers recommendations to effectively groom leaders for America's schools.

The Inadequacies of Principal Training

Formal preparation of school principals usually consists of thirty credits of postbaccalaureate work at a university. For many years, principals have voiced dissatisfaction with university training in preparing them for the realities of their jobs. A 1968 survey of principals found that fewer than 2 percent of elementary principals credited their success as school administrators to their graduate coursework (Department of Elementary School Principals, National Education Association). Recent reports show that principals' sentiments toward their preservice training have not changed significantly. Summarizing the state of affairs in a 1983 policy report, the Southern Regional Education Board (Lynn Cornett) stated that principals' overriding complaint about university training programs is that they are "too theoretical, and do not provide the necessary training to deal with the job."

What is the source of administrators' discontent with their graduate training, and why do university programs fail to adequately prepare aspiring administrators for the principalship?

The central problem appears to be that most university programs present knowledge about school administration, but do not help students develop skills to translate that knowledge into practice. Richard Schmuck (1988) writes:

> Universities . . . have traditionally provided sound academic preparation while offering only minimal attention to transforming theory into practice. Moreover, the academic course work in personnel evaluation, law, business management, clinical supervision, and public relations, although competently presenting technique and technical knowledge, offers little opportunity to use that knowledge in coping with real people in real schools.

Edwin Bridges (1977) suggests that preparatory programs may even promote characteristics that are dysfunctional for those who aspire to be leaders in formal organizations. By comparing the work of graduate students with the work of managers, Bridges provides a lucid analysis of why university programs may not prepare individuals for the realities of leadership.

The Pace of Work

One problem with university training programs is that they do not prepare aspiring administrators to deal with the rapid pace and varied content of principals' work. Drawing on Henry Mintzburg's classical study of managers, *Nature of Managerial Work*, Bridges writes, "Manager's work is characterized by brevity, variety, and fragmentation. The manager's workday is hectic, unpredictable, and riddled with fifty to one hundred different occasions for decisions." Managers are interrupted frequently and often face situations that demand quick decisions.

Academic training programs, on the other hand, require aspiring administrators to spend long hours alone, reading, writing, and contemplating potential solutions to problems. "In comparison with the work pace of managers," Bridges states, "the student's tempo is snail-like. There are few surprises and much time alone." As a result, "the fledgling leader is ill-prepared to handle the accelerated tempo of the managerial role."

Barbara Marrion (1983) studied the experiences of beginning elementary principals in Colorado. The principals spoke to her with considerable emotion about the inadequacies of university training programs in educational administration in preparing them for the pace of the principalship. The following statement was typical: "I wish someone at my university had taken a two-hour class period and told me how really hectic it can be and all the crazy things that can happen."

In my own research of beginning principals in Oregon and Washington (Anderson 1989b), many principals reported fragmented time, feelings of being overwhelmed, and the time demands of the principalship as an entry-year surprise. Consistent with Marrion's findings, many beginners I interviewed were critical of their preservice training for failing to prepare them for the rapid-fire pace of a principal's job.

Dealing with Conflict

A second major problem with university training is that it does not adequately prepare aspiring principals to deal with conflict resolution. The way a manager responds to conflict has a significant effect on his or her relationships with employees and on organizational productivity. Bridges notes that managers use a variety of methods to resolve conflicts. They can engage in win-lose arguing (competition); withdraw or fail to take a position (avoidance); divide gains and seek concessions between parties in conflict (compromise); soothe the parties (accommodation); or confront disagreements and engage in problem solving to find solutions (collaboration).

Leading researchers of leadership and many educators now believe a collaborative style of conflict resolution is likely to foster more productive relationships and enhance the performance of an organization. Bridges suggests that students, however, usually rely on avoidance to resolve conflicts with their classroom teachers. "Collaboration," he writes, "is one of the means least used for resolving conflict."

Communications

A third area of concern is the "character of work-related communications." Administrators typically depend on face-to-face communication to accomplish their work. "Approximately seventy percent of the manager's time involves face-to-face communication with others," Bridges writes. The student, on the other hand, spends more time in reading and writing activities than in work-related personal interactions. Bridges concludes, "There are clearly major discrepancies in the modes of communication that are most relevant to the work of students and that of managers."

Emotions of Work

A final difference between university training and managers' work deals with the emotional content of the workplace. Feelings are not usually examined in graduate training programs, which stress the value of ideas and rationality. "Rarely is the student forced to cope with the emotions of others or to witness situations where people constructively and openly work through their emotional difficulties," Bridges writes. School administrators, on the other hand, deal with emotions constantly. Angry parents, excited students, and aroused staff members are commonplace in a principal's work environment. "Periods of emotional tranquility," Bridges notes, "are punctuated by episodes of emotional turbulence" in a manager's work day.

Beginning principals in my research confirmed Bridges's contention that graduate programs do not provide the type of environment that principals in training need for learning strategies to deal with the emotional demands of the principalship. Many were surprised at the time commitment and the emotion-laden aspects of a principal's job. They also said they felt unprepared to work with concerned and angry parents and teachers. As one principal stated, "I had no training for dealing with it and you need it."

It is unlikely, Bridges concludes, that graduate training programs prepare aspiring administrators for the realities of managerial work. Bridges believes the placid emotional environment of the student may even result in the "trained incapacity" of future leaders. His analysis identifies areas that universities must address to provide relevant training experiences for aspiring principals.

Assessments such as Bridges's, combined with complaints from practitioners and increased awareness of the importance of a principal's leadership, are stirring the demand for changes in methods used by universities and school districts to train administrators. The next section examines recent calls for reform in principal preparation, followed by promising strategies and practices that may improve the preparation process.

Calls for Reform

During the last decade, effective schools research has focused national attention on the importance of a principal's leadership. Virtually all the literature on effective schools points to the critical role that a principal plays in school success. Although correlational studies that have tried to link principal leadership behaviors with student achievement have yielded no significant relationships, effective schools research has contributed to the current practice of zeroing in on the principal as the key agent for achieving educational excellence.

As a result of this recent attention, the preservice training of principals is receiving increased criticism from scholars, national commissions, and principals. Collectively, criticism is aimed at colleges of education and school districts for not providing the field-based experiences necessary for developing outstanding principals.

Kathleen McCormick (1987), citing the 1986 National Governors Association report *Time for Results*, says the certification of principals is currently not based on results, but on educational requirements. "Too often, a candidate's ability to provide instructional leadership does not have to be demonstrated and is not even considered." The National Governors Association report recommends that public schools become more actively involved in the preparation of principals by making clinical experiences a key element in training, certifying, and hiring.

One year later the University Council for Educational Administration (UCEA), in *Leaders for America's Schools*, expanded on these same concerns. The UCEA report states that research reveals a variety of problems related to principal preparation, including lack of collaboration between school districts and universities and lack of preparation programs relevant to the job-related demands encountered by school administrators. Universities, school districts, and professional organizations should cooperate more fully in the preparation of school principals, the report argues.

In 1989, the National Policy Board for Educational Administration published its agenda for reforming the preparation of school administrators. Recommendations included dramatically raising standards for entrance to preparation programs, ensuring the quality of faculty, requiring a doctorate in educational administration for administrators in charge of a school or school system, devoting one full-time year each to academic residency and to field residency, and establishing formal relationships between universities and school districts to create sites for clinical study and field residency. The board also advocated establishing a national professional standards board to administer a national certification examination that states would require candidates for licensure to pass (NPBEA 1989).

In 1990, in its report *Principals for 21st Century Schools*, the National Association of Elementary School Principals (NAESP) reaffirmed that "major surgery" is needed in preparation programs for school principals. In addition to urging more collaboration among colleges, local school districts, professional administration associations, and state education agencies, the report recommends:

- Strengthening prerequisites for entry into principal preparation programs

- Identifying leadership talent early and nurturing its development

- Modifying generic preparation programs to provide greater specialization opportunities for elementary and middle school principals

- Requiring higher education institutions to demonstrate greater commitment to the preparation of principals

In another initiative, NAESP and the National Association of Secondary School Principals jointly created the National Commission for the Principalship to redesign preparation programs and begin plans for a national process of certifying principals. In its report *Principals for Our Changing Schools: Preparation and Certification* (1990), the commission states that it seeks to develop "a new framework for preparing principals based on the realities of the workplace." As a first step toward this goal, the commission developed twenty-one "performance domains" for the principalship that "blend the traditional content-driven curricula with leadership and process skills."

The commission's report recommends that preparation programs interweave clinical experiences with content learning and emphasize the development of *educational leadership*, that is, principals' ability to affect student learning.

Reform of principal preparation must keep pace with the larger school reform movement, which is espousing changes in nearly every aspect of schooling, from what children learn to the way decisions are made to how curriculum is developed and what role parents have in their children's education. All these changes have implications for principals' roles and responsibilities and, hence, their training.

The training required for administrators of restructuring schools is the subject of a report from the U.S. Department of Education's Office of Educational Research and Improvement (Mojkowski 1991) prepared by a study group of OERI's Leadership in Educational Administration Development (LEAD) program center directors. The group concluded that "the values, beliefs, and assumptions that drive restructuring schools are very different from those of traditional schools" and require new forms of leadership that, in turn, suggest the need for new ways of preparing administrators.

The LEAD study group argues that changes in administrator training programs are needed in three areas: the *syllabus*, the *setting*, and the *process*.

> The syllabus needs to blend attention to technical skills, such as resource acquisition and management and information use, with a heavier concentration on people management skills, such as creating dissonance, encouraging risk taking, and forging interdependencies. Training administrators for restructuring schools must prepare them to unleash and direct their powerful people resources toward the mission, goals, and improvement priorities of the schools....

> The most appropriate settings for developing leaders are within schools that are restructuring or planning to restructure. Such contexts provide a fertile environment for blending theory with practice and for forming a learning community within the school....

> The education and training process should 1) integrate learning and work; 2) emphasize action-oriented, problem-solving approaches to training; 3) focus on the development of teams; and 4) be comprehensive, coherent, and continuous. (Mojkowski 1991)

Preparing enlightened administrators who are committed to the continuous development of their intellect and character and who can "lead with their hearts" requires moving beyond training on isolated skills to the cultivation of courage, faith, deep commitment to collaborative action and shared decision-making, and reflection and judgment, the study group concludes.

In an attempt to meet the call for principal preparation reform, educators have tried several promising strategies and practices. Although these strategies are not perfect solutions to improving the training of principals, they are examples of what several institutions are doing to bridge the gap between theoretical concepts of school administration taught in the classroom and the requirements of professional practice in the field.

Promising Training Strategies

To close the gap between classroom and practice, most principal preparation programs now require some type of internship or practicum. A report by the National Association of Secondary School Principals (NASSP), *Performance-Based Preparation of Principals: A Framework for Improvement* (1985), states that field experiences at the conclusion of a student's coursework are often the "sole mechanism of preservice preparation by which the gap is bridged." Although field-based experiences are needed, "such an approach," the report argues, "ignores or makes trivial the breadth of the gap to be spanned."

The NASSP report suggests that a variety of carefully designed bridging procedures must be used in the classroom prior to, or in conjunction with, field experience. These classroom bridging procedures should:

- emanate from appropriate theoretical constructs of the profession and other related disciplines

- provide application in relatively "safe" settings where students can make mistakes and learn from them

- encourage repetitive applications so that students can practice effective behaviors

- place students sufficiently close to the field setting so that the remainder of the transition can be made with a minimum of difficulty

The following sections highlight three classroom bridging procedures: performance simulations, case studies, and games.

Performance Simulations

Performance simulations are one strategy university trainers can use to begin bridging the gap between classroom and field. Simulations recreate situations where the student must quickly formulate strategies to solve problems that school principals typically face. Examples of simulations include inbasket exercises, group activities, stress exercises, and teacher observation simulations.

Originally, simulations were developed for industrial training. Several empirical studies, reported by Bernard Bass (1981), found that managers trained through simulations performed significantly better on supervisory assessments and were perceived by followers as better leaders than those who received a traditional course on leadership principles. Borrowing the simulation idea from business, NASSP developed a number of simulations for its Assessment Center project. In validation studies of NASSP simulations, Neal Schmitt and his colleagues (1982) found high correlations between principals' performance on the simulations and their on-the-job behavior. The greatest drawback of simulations, according to NASSP, is that "too few excellent simulations are available, making repeated applications unfeasible."

Case Studies

Another effort to make classroom preparation reflect actual experience of principals uses case studies rich in descriptions and contextual details of actual situations. These case studies are designed to help aspiring principals develop analytical, problem-solving, and decision-making skills. According to Vivian Clark (1986), case studies capture the "brevity, variety, and fragmentation in the principalship and demonstrate the attempts by various principals to meet these demands of the job."

Clark recommends that those involved in training principals should use case studies for class discussions. Case studies help both trainers and students to examine the basis for decisions and their effectiveness. They also help students to analyze how they might handle situations. She concludes that although "case studies do not provide panaceas for training principals, ... they can be a very useful training tool and should not be overlooked."

Games

Organizational, institutional, and business games are a third bridging strategy. Trainees make sequential decisions and are responsible for the results. During games, participants experience success and failure more fully than in other types of simulations. Wilderness labs are an example of a training game that has achieved widespread recognition and use by corporations such as AT&T, Xerox, General Electric, and Marriott.

Although wilderness labs have not been extensively used in education, a new principal training program at the University of Oregon does incorporate this training activity. According to Richard Schmuck, the program's director, the focus of Oregon's wilderness lab is on leadership development and team building. The lab takes place on a "Ropes Course" owned and operated by a 4-H organization near Salem, Oregon.

"Aspiring principals take on a series of structured mental and physical challenges designed as metaphors for professional challenges in a school," says Schmuck (1988).

> Success depends not on physical strength or athletic skill, but on a team's ability to solve problems creatively, allocate diverse resources effectively, maintain commitment of team members, and develop support networks. After each challenge, the participants as individuals and the teams reflect on the process: What contributed to team effectiveness? What fueled or took away energy and commitment of individuals? How might we apply what we're learning to the school? By the end of the weekend, insights from the woods are translated into action plans for the school.

According to the NASSP report, university training programs do not use performance simulations, case studies, games, or other classroom bridging procedures very extensively.

> Most programs use them only in minimal ways. No program, perhaps, uses them to an optimum degree. Some of this neglect is attributable to the small number and variety of bridging procedures. A greater proportion of the problem may be due to lack of recognition

14

that performance-based learning is important for sufficient transfer of theory to practice.

NASSP recommends an extensive professional effort to develop more and better classroom bridging procedures, to disseminate them, and to incorporate them into preparation programs.

In addition to classroom bridging procedures, various field-based experiences are also recommended for the preservice training of principals. The following section features three types of useful field-based experiences: course-based field activities, practicums, and internships.

Course-Based Field Activities

It is helpful for aspiring administrators to engage in fieldwork that directly explores various aspects of the principal's role. In course-based field activities, trainers require students to complete assignments, such as conducting field interviews and observations, that add a practical dimension to academic coursework. Examples of course-based assignments are as follows:

- observing a school board meeting, negotiations sessions, student discipline hearing, or faculty meeting

- interviewing administrators on a specific topic such as developing a building budget, bringing about a change in a program, or designing a staff inservice plan

- observing and then conducting a teacher observation and postconference

- attending a regional or state principal conference

- interviewing a school board member or political leader on issues central to education

The best field activities are those that enable students to see how theoretical or technical aspects of school administration can be applied. In addition, trainers in effective programs teach students various observation and interview recording techniques prior to their field-based assignments. Finally, they assist students in carefully analyzing information collected in the field. Without critical analysis and reflection, the activities are primarily passive in nature and may not help students develop useful insights.

Practica

Practica can also help aspiring administrators begin to translate theory into practice. A practicum is usually a significant project, at least one semester in duration, in which students demonstrate administrative skills. In exemplary training programs, the student is accountable for planning, implementing, and evaluating one or more projects.

Practica should occur not only near the end of students' university training sequence, but throughout the training period. With this approach, universities and school districts can use the practicum as part of a career guidance plan that allows those interested in administration to "test the waters" before deciding to pursue administration as a career. The current practice in most universities is to schedule practica near the end of preservice education. Unfortunately, this occurs after students have already invested so much time and money in their training that a brief exposure to reality in the field is unlikely to alter their career paths.

A second criterion for a successful practicum experience is that university faculty members and school district administrators work together to closely supervise and provide helpful feedback on students' projects. According to the NASSP, university supervisors, school district administrators, and peers need to carefully analyze and constructively critique students' practicum projects. "The ability of the student to receive and utilize relevant criticism," the report argues, should be "one of the criteria applied in assessing practicum outcomes."

A final criterion for an exemplary practicum experience requires students to bring about a change in some aspect of a school's structures, norms, or traditional procedures, as they work directly with people involved in the school. Thus, relevant practicum assignments will probably require some release time from an aspirant's regular duties. University faculty and school administrators should also provide students with information and ideas on successful change strategies and carefully guide aspiring administrators through a change process. Examples of appropriate practicum projects include:

- initiating a new norm, structure, or procedure for inservice training in a school

- observing and improving a school's discipline or attendance procedure

- developing a student, teacher, or volunteer recognition program

- improving curriculum articulation within a school or initiating a new instructional strategy with staff in a curricular area

Internships

If carefully designed and supervised, internships most closely approximate the scope and complexity of an actual position. The idea of internships, which give prospective principals a chance to try their hands at real-life school administration, is not new; full-time internships are, however, still the exception rather than the rule. The Carnegie Foundation for the Advancement of Teaching favored extensive internship experiences for principal hopefuls in its 1983 study *High School: A Report on Secondary Education in America*. Carnegie's president, former U.S. Commissioner of Education Ernest L. Boyer, recommends a one-year administrative internship in which the candidate works closely, on a full-time basis, with an experienced, successful principal.

In his 1983 landmark study *A Place Called School*, John Goodlad also called for lengthy internship experiences. "It is simply not established procedure in the educational system to identify and groom cadres of the most promising prospects for top positions, as is the case with IBM, for example." Goodlad believes school districts must be willing to make an investment designed to pay future dividends. An example would be to create one or more internships as assistant principals and to schedule potential candidates for paid, two-year study programs carefully planned to balance academic study and on-the-job experience.

Internships will not produce outstanding leaders unless they are carefully designed, supervised, and scheduled over a sufficient period. On the basis of his study of beginning principals, John Daresh (1987a) believes that districts' failure to grant release time for aspiring administrators may be a significant roadblock to effective training experiences. He states that most internships and practica consist of

> synthetic situations where aspiring principals, in most cases full-time teachers unable to get district support and approval for release time, find some quasi-admin-

17

istrative tasks that can be performed during the time that is not assigned during the school day to teaching or other duties. As a result, people are being prepared to serve as instructional leaders by spending five to ten hours per week supervising bus loadings, calling the homes of truant students, filling out forms for the central office or the state department of education, or devising new student handbooks. These activities are, no doubt, useful for the smooth operation of a school, and many practicing administrators are engaged in these activities every day. However, to rely on projects such as these to give anyone a clear picture of the multifaceted nature of most principals' jobs is truly ludicrous.

Daresh also suggests that the assumption behind such training—competence comes from practical experience—may be false. "Simply assuming that one learns by doing practical things is an incorrect assumption," he writes. Daresh believes that aspiring administrators need to spend a great deal of time reflecting on and analyzing the skills they learn in the field and the activities in which they are engaged. "Practice without reflection," he notes, "is not of great value to learning anything." Thus, Daresh recommends that trainers guide students through a reflective learning cycle to improve students' administrative abilities and insights. "This guidance takes time and requires a true concern for the learner as an individual," notes Daresh. Unfortunately, he states, "preparation of administrative candidates in many universities is not a very personalized process."

Several university-school partnerships are beginning to address the shortcomings of past internships. For example, Georgia's Bibb County Public School System developed an exemplary internship program in cooperation with the University of Georgia. According to Thomas Hagler and his colleagues (1987), aspiring administrators in the program spend an entire year in a full- time internship. In addition to working full-time under the supervision of experienced administrators, the interns observe other principals in the district, attend monthly seminars conducted by the superintendent and his staff, and meet twice a month with the university coordinator. Interns also attend bimonthly seminars with their peers where they share frustrations and triumphs, pose problems and offer solutions, reflect on their activities, compare perceptions and experiences, and develop support networks.

Interns at Bibb County also enroll in a sequence of five-credit university courses. These courses, intended to link coursework to intern activities, include Introduction to Supervision, Administration of the School Curriculum, and Public School Business Administration. University faculty members and school district administrators also work together to carefully design and closely supervise each intern's program.

Similar university-school district intern partnerships have been implemented in Alaska (McDermott 1984), Texas (Erlandson and Gonzalez 1988), Utah (Wasden, Muse, and Ovard 1987), Oregon (Schmuck 1988), and Kentucky (Cline and Richardson 1988), to name a few. References to these intern programs are included in the bibliography.

School Systems Invest in Training

Although our focus so far has been on university training programs, probably the most crucial ingredient in preparing capable school leaders is the school district. Without the financial and emotional support of senior school administrators and school boards, the prospects for "growing a healthy crop" of new principals who can effectively lead our nation's schools during the upcoming decades is highly unlikely.

Exemplary training programs are costly. According to Catherine Baltzell and Robert Dentler (1983), "The extent to which the school system invests in the preparation of principals is an index to other aspects of system quality." Baltzell and Dentler found that many districts are not willing to make such an investment, and, consequently, do not have a qualified pool of potential candidates from which to choose.

Baltzell and Dentler cite some districts that do provide the necessary training for prospective principals. For example, Maryland's Montgomery County Public Schools began its leadership transformation efforts twenty years ago. In its Administrative Training Program, potential principals enroll in a ten-week afterwork course on leadership. Graduates may then opt for a second eighteen-week, three-credit course in administrative leadership, which includes skill development.

After candidates complete this two-part sequence, senior administrators review all performance and related educational

19

records of applicants and rank them by points. Highest scoring candidates who are still interested in the principalship are then invited to "Administrative Competence Seminars," where their interpersonal skills, communication and conceptual skills, and group leadership skills are formally assessed by a panel of senior administrators. Candidates are reranked according to points awarded for their performance on each of the activities in the competence seminars.

Top-ranked individuals are then given one-year internships as full-time assistant principals. Under the guidance of successful administrators, interns obtain experience in such areas as instructional leadership, staff and pupil personnel management, community involvement, and professional growth. At monthly seminars attended by interns and their supervisory team, interns present an analysis of their log of daily activities and share a selected activity for group analysis and discussion. Each intern also completes a needs assessment on his or her strengths and weaknesses. The assessment is used to develop an individual training plan designed to extend the intern's knowledge and skill in such areas as leadership, management, and supervision.

Training programs like the one in Montgomery County Schools are highly desirable but very rare, according to the U.S. Department of Education report on principal selection. However, Baltzell and Dentler found some districts that are beginning to meet the challenge of training future school leaders. My own research in Oregon and Washington identified districts that are making the necessary investments of time and money to groom capable principals.

A Northwest district that I investigated (1988a) provides a three-year internship for aspiring school administrators. The interns rub shoulders with all administrators and fully participate in various aspects of school administration either as an administrative assistant to the superintendent or an intern principal of a small school within the district. The district compensates interns with wages above a regular teacher's salary but below that of a principal.

Under the tutelage of the superintendent, the intern serves as his assistant and has responsibility for dealing with community relations, overseeing student and employee hearings, chairing ad hoc committees, troubleshooting for the superintendent, and assisting in policy development. The assistant also works closely with building principals and central office supervisors on various

20

issues and attends all principal and superintendent cabinet meetings.

The rotation of the principalship in a small elementary school serves as another three-year internship. Under the mentorship and supervision of a veteran principal, the intern receives a full-time training opportunity. Such internships provide just what national leaders are recommending to train capable school principals. Hopefully, more districts will begin to realize that the training of capable leaders must begin long before they are needed.

The 'Leadership for Excellence' Program

The current movement to enhance the competence of the nation's principal corps would be shortsighted if it focused only on the preservice stage of training. Principals who have been in their positions for one, five, or even twenty years can still benefit from professional development activities that build or reinforce essential leadership skills.

One highly practical program designed to enhance principal leadership has been developed by the Northwest Regional Educational Laboratory* (1988). Leadership for Excellence (LFE) is a systematic professional development program that focuses on actions school administrators can take to make their schools more effective. A school district could also use the program to train staff members who aspire to become principals.

To develop the program, staff at NWREL first reviewed the literature on effective schools to ascertain what successful principals do to improve their schools' ability to foster learning in all children. Based on their examination of the research, five key areas, or strands, of principal leadership were identified. Workshop materials were developed to address each of the five identified strands: Vision Building, School Climate and Culture, Improving Instruction, Implementing Curriculum, and Monitoring School Progress.

Material in each strand, which has been pilot-tested and field-tested, is presented during a series of three four- to six-hour workshops. All five strands include cooperative learning exer-

---

*The author acknowledges the contribution of Linda Lumsden to this section.

cises, extensive background reading materials, research overviews, action planning, group discussions, small group exercises, and evaluations.

LFE is designed so that the five areas of concentration, or strands, may be purchased individually or collectively. The cost per strand of having LFE presented varies according to the number of participants and where the presentation will take place. NWREL's School Improvement Director, Bob Blum, who developed the materials along with Nancey Olson, notes that "anyone interested in principal training can buy and use any or all of the five strands as they see fit." The primary objective of the developers, states Blum, "is to get the materials to the people who have the responsibility for enhancing the skills of practicing principals and preparing those aspiring to become principals."

A brief overview of the content of each strand reveals the highly practical nature of this program:

Vision Building—Since effective leadership requires having a clear understanding of the school's mission and where it is headed, participants in this strand carefully examine and clarify their personal values, beliefs, and expectations about the purposes of education. They engage their entire staffs in a similar process of developing a unified vision for the future of their schools. In the last workshop, participants learn and try out ways of communicating their vision through both formal and informal means.

School Climate and Culture—Participants learn about factors affecting school culture and climate and discover how these factors differ in highly effective and less effective schools. A variety of tools for assessing school culture and climate are examined and participants gain practical experience by conducting an assessment in their own school. They learn cooperative decision-making strategies, engage their staff in evaluating the current status of their school climate and culture, and reach consensus on one or two areas of culture or climate to improve. Participants also learn about planning methods that can help them implement selected culture and climate characteristics that have the potential for increasing student success and improving working conditions and relationships among staff. The final workshop in this strand concentrates on reviewing research on change and implementing innovations

Improving Instruction—Improving Teaching Together is the theme of this strand. The first workshop is devoted to defining

22

effective teaching and building a framework for using research to improve instruction. Procedures for using video as a tool for improving instruction are featured in the second workshop. The final session focuses on staff development practices, including peer assistance, that have been shown to lead to better teaching. Participants learn the importance of engaging their staff in applying the findings of research on effective teaching.

Implementing Curriculum—In the initial workshop, participants examine the components of a comprehensive curriculum improvement cycle and determine their role in the process. Next, participants work with their staffs across grade levels and departments to clearly define instructional priorities and timelines. By the end of the third session, participants should be able to develop a monitoring system that will assess student achievement in various program areas and evaluate the degree to which teachers are implementing the written curriculum.

Monitoring School Progress—Indicators of and procedures for monitoring schoolwide performance are discussed in the first session. At the building level, principals then work with staff to create guidelines for using data on student outcomes, noting advantages and disadvantages of possible uses and discussing precautions that may need to be taken. The second workshop covers collecting information and organizing it into a school profile. Emphasis is on student performance, which includes achievement, social behavior, and attitude data. The third workshop shows how staff analysis of these data provides information for use in setting school goals through consensus-building activities. It also shows participants how to construct plans for systematically examining staff use of effective schooling practices.

It is clear that preparation programs for twenty-first-century principals need immediate attention and support. School districts and universities must commit themselves, both financially and emotionally, to improving the preservice preparation of America's future school leaders. This chapter concludes with recommendations that should be considered in designing new principal preparation training activities.

Recommendations for Training

1. Develop hands-on preservice training activities. Universities, school districts, and professional associations of school administrators must work cooperatively to develop and provide additional practical hands-on training opportunities for aspiring school principals. All these groups are stakeholders in the process. With input from veteran practitioners, university trainers should design coursework that, at a minimum, emphasizes effective instructional practices and the role of the principal in instructional leadership, effective communication and interpersonal skills, conflict management skills, change strategies, school culture and climate, technological applications to management and instruction, building-level budgeting (versus only state and school district budgeting), and staff supervision and evaluation, to name a few.

University training should not only include conceptual and technical knowledge, but also provide simulation exercises that enable aspirants to apply the theoretical knowledge of the university classroom to real school-related situations. Performance simulations, inbasket exercises, games, course-based field activities, and case studies are some of the methods trainers can use to help aspiring principals bridge the gap between being a graduate student and functioning as a school principal.

2. Design numerous practica experiences. Practica, in which aspiring principals perform significant projects in a school, should occur frequently and throughout administrative preparation programs, not only near the end of students' training. Opportunities to "test the waters" throughout a preparation sequence will allow neophytes the opportunity to refine their administrative skills while actually working with people in schools. To be successful, ongoing and constructive feedback must be provided by university supervisors, school district administrators, and classmates so that students can reflect on, grow, and learn from their practicum experiences.

3. Provide full-time internships. The internship should be a critical part of the training prospective school leaders undergo. To be effective, internships must be of sufficient duration and intensity to approximate the complex conditions that aspiring administrators will encounter in an actual principalship. A duration of one-half year is a minimum and one or two years is ideal. Part-day or part-week internships do not provide a realistic view of what occurs in a typical full-time position. Thus, school districts must make a significant financial commitment to grooming the most capable principals.

It is also vital that school district supervisors spend a great deal of time guiding and supervising the intern in a collegial fashion. Furthermore, university and school district supervisors must work together to plan and guide students' intern experiences. For the internship to be a productive and relevant training experience, a well-designed working agreement should be developed. It should clarify in concrete terms the expectations, rights, responsibilities, and functions of the intern, university supervisor, and field supervisor and should include a list of required activities to assist the aspirant in dealing with the complexities of principal work.

4. Facilitate reflective seminars. Universities and school districts should organize well-designed seminars, held on a monthly or semimonthly basis. The seminars should bring together university faculty, field supervisors, interns, and successful school leaders to reflect on the interns' experiences, to solve problems, and to make plans for additional learning experiences. Support groups and networks among interns and practicing school administrators should be an outgrowth of the monthly seminars.

Finally, school districts can encourage their administrative staff to take part in the activities of state and national principals' associations, which offer training seminars as well as a network for renewal and professional development.

Effective training programs are, of course, only the first step in developing capable principals; recruitment, selection, induction, and evaluation are other essential components in a comprehensive system that trains, obtains, and retains the most capable school leaders.

PRINCIPALS

HOW TO TRAIN, RECRUIT, SELECT, INDUCT, AND EVALUATE LEADERS FOR AMERICA'S SCHOOLS

RECRUITING AND SELECTING PRINCIPALS

Recruiting and selecting capable candidates for school leadership positions may be the most important task facing superintendents and school boards in the next few years. With predictions that more than half of current principals will retire during the next decade, districts have a golden opportunity to hire many outstanding newcomers. As a senior personnel administrator in a suburban Northwest school district said, sophisticated recruitment and selection processes are now a necessity. "We are in a very competitive business, and we must make sure, through our process, we don't miss the best candidates."

Unfortunately, many districts recruit and select principals in a haphazard fashion, often overlooking the most capable candidates. Goodlad (in an interview by Sally Zakariya 1983) said that the recruiting and hiring of principals is "to say the least casual. Most new principals are plucked out of the classroom in June and plunged into the job soon after."

Robert Dentler likewise believes the principal recruitment and selection process is "ridden with chance" and often does not conform to sound policy. As he told Zakariya,

> In most places, principal recruitment and selection still
> operates on the buddy system. Without changes in the
> integrity and vitality of the selection process, the ablest
> educational leaders may never turn their faces towards
> the principalship.

The recruitment and selection of outstanding principals is too important to be left to chance. Patronage, favoritism, or familiarity should not edge out merit. Goodlad, Dentler, and many other observers recommend that school districts begin grooming future principals long before they are needed, thereby developing a pool of qualified candidates from which to select the brightest and best. This chapter assesses problems in the recruitment and selection of principals, describes exemplary screening and selection techniques, and offers guidelines to assist school districts in selecting the most capable leaders for our nation's schools.

A Limited Pool of Capable Candidates

Although the pool of principal candidates is large—many individuals possess the required certification—there is reason to believe the number of "highly capable" applicants may be dwindling. Through interviews with school leaders for *The Executive Educator*, Kathleen McCormick (1987) found a growing concern about a pending shortage of "rising stars" for the principalship. Scott Thompson, then executive director of the 42,000-member NASSP, told McCormick, "We don't have enough top-notch people to fill the jobs."

Superintendent Frank Cleary of Binghamton, New York, told McCormick, "I don't see as many people coming up through the system who have the burning desire to climb the administrative ladder." One reason, Cleary explained, is that teaching itself is becoming a more attractive career: salaries are improving and teachers are being given greater control over and responsibility for what happens in the classroom. "Teachers spend more time looking at the pros and cons of administration," he says. Because of the high cost of moving and complications resulting from two-career families, he added, "the list of cons outweighs the pros, unless you can stay in the same district."

As discouraging as all this might sound, leaders in education do agree that opportunities for talented and dedicated newcomers, including women and minorities, will increase in the next few years. Effie Jones, associate executive director of the American Association of School Administrators, told McCormick, "There are plenty of talented women and minorities who are now certified to take administrative positions." Scott Thompson agrees "there are more strong women candidates than ever before." In the end, says McCormick, the exodus of experienced principals "might be just the window of opportunity that women and ethnic minorities have been waiting for. That is, if today's school leaders take the initiative to help train them."

Ways to Expand the Applicant Pool

Several studies call for school districts to make a concerted effort to expand the pool of qualified principal applicants. Outside recruitment, indistrict training programs, career ladders, and internships are ways for districts to accomplish this.

Outside Recruitment

According to Goodlad (1983), "School districts would be well advised—and perhaps should be required—to select, for posts available, from a pool of qualified applicants extending far beyond district lines." This procedure does not nullify a district's investment in principal preparation, he adds. "With all districts similarly engaged in the process, interest from investments would be shared."

Frequently school districts restrict their vacancy announcements to narrow geographic areas. The U.S. Department of Education's *Principal Selection Guide* (1987) criticizes this practice and recommends that

> announcements should be placed in large circulation newspapers in cities within a 500-mile radius of the vacancy. If the district is itself in a large city, the search committee might advertise the opening in similar cities. To avoid becoming too ingrown, search committees should advertise in principal and superintendent newsletters, in education journals, and in the publications or at the conferences of professional associations. There are many options, but the most important thing is to avoid a narrow search that ends too soon.

Outside recruitment does not consist of simply advertising vacancies beyond local boundaries; it also focuses on finding and targeting individuals in other districts who are perceived as highly desirable candidates. According to Baltzell and Dentler, "If all goes well, the outsider is ultimately brought in. However, it is usually an outsider with a firm inside connection to the network." Districts with limited pools of applicants rarely recruit in such a manner.

School districts would also be well advised to work closely with other districts, state administration associations, women's educational administration associations, and groups of minority educators to encourage and recruit applicants from all segments of the population. As one superintendent who has been particularly successful at recruiting capable female administrators says, "We are attempting to recruit our leadership from the whole population, not just half of it."

Career Ladders

Career ladders are another means by which to expand the pool of qualified applicants, but, again, use of this method tends to be the exception rather than the rule. Career ladders can include positions for curriculum and staff development specialists, head teachers, department chairs, deans, and assistant principals.

Although career ladders are a way to test applicants' leadership abilities, many times districts do not provide the individuals occupying these positions with the diverse experiences that are necessary for grooming outstanding principals. This is especially true of the assistant principal position, as James Lindsay (1985) notes:

> Too few assistant principals are groomed for higher positions; they receive narrow, theoretical training, and the on-the-job experience they have is just as narrow. Usually, an assistant principal is treated as a single-facet administrator—prepared, for instance, to be only a disciplinarian or only a director of activities. As a result, most assistant principals learn only a few of the many job skills they need to be good principals.

Lindsay believes in providing assistant principals with experience in all facets of building administration to strengthen a district's pool of trained and tested principal candidates. Principals themselves, Lindsay notes, play an important role in this training process:

> As a principal, you owe it to your assistants to help them develop into well-rounded, qualified professionals who are prepared to move into new, challenging positions. There's no magic to the process. All it requires is dedication and the willingness to make school administration a superior form of continuing education.

Internships and Training Programs

As noted in chapter 1, internships and district training

programs are examples of methods used to attract, train, and expand the applicant pool. To be effective, teachers must perceive these training opportunities as accessible, open, valuable, and professional. According to Baltzell and Dentler, candidates in exemplary districts have a much greater sense of passing through a sequence of ever-narrowing gates as they are "weeded out" through credible training programs and internships.

One Northwest district's recruitment and training program provides a practical example of what school districts can do to improve the pool of principal candidates. In January 1987, the David Douglas School District in Portland, Oregon (with an 1987-88 enrollment of approximately 6,000 students in 11 schools), launched its STAR (Selecting and Training Administrative Recruits) program for identifying, recruiting, and training prospective principals from within the district's teacher corps.

Of STAR's three phases, the first involves a series of ten weekly classes, held at the conclusion of the school day, about educational administration. Each class, taught by a team of David Douglas administrators, covers different aspects of administration relevant to David Douglas. Training focuses on the practical realities of the principalship, addressing both the frustrations and the joys. Topics are grouped according to four roles of the administrator:

> *Member of the administrative team.* An opening session includes presentations by the superintendent and principals from the elementary, middle, and high school levels on the administrative team structure in the district and each member's responsibilities.

> *Educational program coordinator.* Directors of programs such as special education, instructional materials, music, and PE outline their respective roles and relationship with district principals.

> *Instructional leader.* Principals and the curriculum director focus on components of an instructional leader such as research, classroom strategies, staff development, evaluation of programs, and skills in dealing with people.

> *Building manager.* Supervisors from business, transportation, food service, and data processing discuss their interaction with school principals and the principal's extensive involvement in these various areas of district operations.

Other sessions in phase 1 include the administrator as disciplinarian, personnel manager, community relations specialist, financial wizard, and first-year rookie. All sessions encourage active class participation by means of questions and answers, brainstorming sessions, and small-group work.

Phase 2 of STAR consists of a week-long practicum experience, based on a plan that each participant designs in phase 1. During this second phase, mentor relationships are formed between participants and administrators. Interested candidates also attend an assessment center for evaluation and training.

In the final phase, the district establishes formal internships with building principals for interested and successful candidates. In addition, the district offers a series of workshops in the second year of the program that explore, in greater depth, topics in educational leadership.

Although STAR is designed to provide David Douglas teachers with information about becoming a principal in their own district, participants become involved in the program for several reasons. Some are in the process of getting their administrative credentials and want to get the David Douglas perspective on what they have learned. For those who are undecided about going into administration, the STAR program provides participants with more information on which to base that decision. The program also sends the message to employees that the district values their competence and is interested in supporting their investigation of and preparation for school administration.

Pattern for Effective Recruitment

In sum, aggressive school districts do not leave the identification and recruitment of outstanding principals to chance.

Long before vacancies arise, they identify a pool of potential leaders and develop a "pipeline" to the principalship. District training programs, internships, and the assignment of teachers to various leadership roles are various ways of grooming a cadre of capable candidates. Better yet, a training and internship program that welcomes women and minority candidates can help to equalize opportunities for these groups.

Aggressive districts not only train people from within the district for future principalships, they also recruit outside the district, often advertising widely in college job placement bulletins and professional organizations' newsletters. Targeting talented individuals in other districts and helping them gain access to the district's network is another recruitment strategy. Districts increase their odds of finding the best candidates when they welcome a large number of applicants.

Selecting Principals

The selection process is central in hiring the most capable principals. As we will see, several studies suggest that many school districts may not select the best candidates. There are two possible explanations for this: (1) districts' vacancy announcements and selection criteria are nonspecific, and (2) districts use inadequate screening and selection techniques. This section suggests ways to strengthen vacancy announcements, selection criteria, screening and assessment methods, and interview procedures.

Vacancy Announcements

Principal selection begins with the declaration of a vacancy. Far too often, vacancy announcements, especially in large districts, do not specify the particular school where the opening exists. Rather, the announcements call for applications for the principalship in general. Although most districts hire principals to serve in various schools during their tenure, there are good reasons to specify the particular school where a vacancy occurs. Districts are more likely to attract good candidates when vacancy announcements list information concerning the special needs and characteristics of a school. In addition, selectors can increase the chances of selecting the right person for the job when they assess and match candidates' skills and leadership styles with the particular needs of a school.

Laura Fliegner (1987) argues that districts should provide the following types of information in vacancy announcements:

- needs to be accomplished by whomever fills the position

- important characteristics of the existing staff

- students' family background, cultures, extracurricular concerns, and feelings about school

- information about other executives in the school system

A district I investigated provides a good example of such an announcement. In an attractive announcement brochure, the district enumerates details about the particular opening, including characteristics of the school such as projected enrollment, makeup of student population, and types of facilities; a profile of the school staff; and information on the community, school superintendent, and school board. In addition, the brochure lists several required and preferred qualifications, skills, and traits the district wants candidates to have. Finally, the announcement includes information on salary, benefits, and days worked per year.

Because more frequent assignment changes may be necessary in larger school systems, it may not be feasible for them to provide as much specific information about vacancies. They may have to develop more comprehensive, general standards for announcing principal vacancies. This may have undesired effects, for as Baltzell and Dentler warn, "When the resulting set of standards becomes too general, the generalities detract from the vacancy pool and from screening efforts."

Selection Criteria

The best districts take the time and care necessary to clearly define and articulate what they are looking for in a principal and how they will determine whether a candidate meets selection criteria. Developing clear criteria increases a district's likelihood of hiring a top-notch principal. Exemplary districts, therefore, decide in advance what kind of data they will use to appraise candidates. Lorri Manasse (1983) argues that

> school districts need to make more explicit their criteria for selecting principals. If they are to move toward an instructional component in their definition of principal effectiveness, they need to clearly articulate selection and evaluation criteria that reflect that definition.

Baltzell and Dentler (1983) agree:

> Even when a district clearly aligns a vacancy with a specific school, many districts do not spell out criteria pertinent to educational leadership such as experience with program planning, budgeting, staff development and evaluation, plant management, or community relations.

The following criteria, enumerated in one school district's principal vacancy announcement, provide an example of the kind of specificity needed. Each district, of course, must develop criteria that reflect the qualifications they seek.

Required Qualifications
- A record of exemplary teaching experiences
- Outstanding performance as a school improvement leader
- A record of successful community relations
- Demonstrated leadership in clinical supervision

Preferred Qualifications
- ITIP training and supervisory experiences
- Staff development experiences
- Knowledge of effective schools research
- Leadership experience as a principal or administrator
- Completion of NASSP Assessment Center simulations

Personal Traits
- A sensitivity to people
- A rapport with students
- The ability to inspire colleagues and students
- The ability to write and speak articulately
- A sense of humor
- The ability to encourage and use the information and opinions of diverse groups in decision-making
- Strong organizational skills

Many districts postpone the definition of such criteria until a candidate pool has been formed and review has begun, say Baltzell and Dentler. They claim that "this lack of criterial specificity opens the way for widespread reliance on localistic notions of fit or image." For example, many districts in their study had a deeply held image of a "good" principal or a "top" candidate or "just what they were looking for." But instead of hiring a candidate based on skills or merit, these districts relied more on how a candidate would fit into the district and maintain the existing system. Hiring officials' perceptions were influenced by their assessment of a candidate's physical presence, projections of a certain self-confidence and assertiveness, and embodiment of community values and district's methods of operation.

Baltzell and Dentler found that districts employing exemplary selection practices give priority to "merit" over "fit." In the districts that employed this approach to selection, selection teams looked for principals who could institute effective change, not merely maintain the status quo. Based on their desire to hire effective change agents, these districts also used a well-defined set of criteria to systematically sort and rank candidates before selecting finalists for interviews. Without such screening and selection criteria, it is less likely that districts will hire the most capable principal.

Screening

Screening typically involves two steps. First, the personnel office screens resumés and applications of candidates who meet specified certification and experience standards. Next, there is a more formalized paper screening of eligible candidates who pass the initial screening. It is at this stage that many districts begin to falter.

Fliegner (1987) believes school districts need to create comprehensive job descriptions and selection criteria, obtaining feedback from staff members, students, community members, and administrators. Next, she says, "A district must develop a screening scheme and standardized ranking system by which screeners can systematically judge each applicant's file against their predetermined standards."

Exemplary districts have screeners who conduct blind ratings of each candidate by assigning a numerical score to each candidate's application and reference documentation. Assuming districts competently handle these important preliminary steps, the issue of who screens is another problem.

Who Screens?

In his treatise *Victims of Groupthink*, social psychologist S. L. (Irving) Janis (1972) uses the term "groupthink"

> to refer to a mode of thinking that people engage in
> when they are deeply involved in a cohesive in-group,

when the members' strivings for unanimity override their motivations to realistically appraise alternative courses of action.

In the districts they studied, Baltzell and Dentler note that the "groupthink" tendency often occurs when a small, close-knit group of senior administrators do all the screening. Over time, they lose their ability to correct each other's errors and judgment. The researchers say that

> without some other participation (parents, teachers, principals, or students) screening looses its external credibility. It appears to take place in a way no one can attest to as trustworthy or well executed, except by the same team members.

I interviewed an assistant superintendent of personnel in a medium-size suburban district who said the inclusion of building principals and teachers on the screening and interview committee allows the district to "get various perspectives on all dimensions of what a principal candidate should be." This participation also makes the process fair and curtails "a 'good-old-boy' network where a favorite of the central office administration is preselected," he said.

Participation of teachers, principals, parents, and even students on screening committees is one way a district can combat the "groupthink" syndrome. Exemplary schools rely heavily on the participation of school-based as well as district-level administration and staff for screening and selecting principals.

Assessment Centers

A promising option for screening potential principal candidates is the assessment center. Using an idea borrowed from the business world, the NASSP began the first assessment center in 1975. It is one of the fastest growing approaches in education for identifying and screening prospective candidates, who participate in a variety of simulations.

The assessment center helps districts pinpoint potential principals' specific strengths and weaknesses in a dozen job-related areas: problem analysis, judgment, organizational ability, decisiveness, leadership, sensitivity, stress tolerance, oral communication, written communication, range of interests, personal motivation, and educational values. According to Zakariya (1983),

"The result is a 12-dimensional profile of each candidate, which can be used as a prescription for professional development as well as a screening device."

Unfortunately, the cost of assessment centers deters many districts from participating. As Dentler told Zakariya, "They are fairly expensive and cumbersome to put into place. People are looking for shortcuts, and there just aren't any." No shortcuts may, in fact, be a fitting epitaph for the old-fashioned wink-and-nod school of picking principals. "When you spend time and effort on selecting good principals," says Dentler, "you get both short-term and long-term payoffs—not just good leaders, but good system operations."

Written Assessments

Districts that use highly effective selection strategies also require some type of written communication as part of the screening and selection process. Writing assignments help screeners assess a candidate's philosophical views and communication skills. In one district I investigated, candidates are asked to respond in essay form to a series of pertinent questions. Examples of these questions are as follows:

1. What are some key descriptors of leadership and management? Give some examples of how you personally have used these elements to advantage.

2. Entrenched faculties and organizations can often be resistant to change. What processes will you employ in moving a school organization toward your envisioned change?

3. As a principal new to our district, you choose to introduce yourself to the staff by providing working definitions of *teaching* and *learning*. How do you introduce yourself?

4. Recently the local paper editorialized that only after parents got involved in the schools has education improved. How will you direct into productive channels the energies of an active school community?

Having applicants provide several short written essays "gives us a good idea of how candidates express themselves in writing: how they think," a senior administrator told me. In addition, "We have a strong feeling about the use of language as a mark of an educated person. Candidates have told us that our written exercise forced them to focus their philosophy into a succinct statement and quickly get to the crux of key issues."

The Interview

The interview is the most widely used and most influential selection technique in hiring decisions. Yet the interview, if used incorrectly or used as the sole basis for hiring, is neither valid nor reliable. According to Mary Cihak Jensen (1986):

> Typically, the interview is unstructured, lasts less than one hour, and is highly influenced by first impressions, appearance, nonverbal behavior, and conversational skills.

Some studies suggest that interviewers may arrive at their decision to hire or reject an applicant within the first five minutes of the interview. The remainder of the interview can become merely an effort to confirm initial impressions. According to E.C. Webster (1982), "that early decision can be biased by what business calls the 'old school tie syndrome', the tendency of interviewers to prefer applicants similar to themselves."

Districts using sophisticated selection techniques choose principals who tend not to fit the stereotype of the tall, white, middle-aged, male principal. Instead, says Dentler, in exemplary systems, "we found more women, blacks, hispanics and Asian-Americans. And more short people." In other words, selection in these districts seems to be based not on physical attractiveness, personality, fit, or first impressions, but on merit. How do you determine a candidate's merit? The much maligned interview process does hold some promise.

Selecting Interviewers

Districts can improve the interview process by recognizing that not all people are equally adept at interviewing candidates. Jensen lists five qualifications for teacher interviewers that are applicable to principal selectors as well. Districts should select interviewers possessing these qualifications:

- alertness to cues

- ability to make fine distinctions, perceive accurately
- ability to make immediate and accurate records
- willingness to use criteria established by the organization
- ability to suppress biases

Determining the individuals to involve in the interview is an important decision districts must make. Several studies advise using parents, teachers, and principals on the interview team to acquire different perspectives, to create a sense of ownership in the process, and to gain support for the candidate who is finally selected. In exemplary districts, superintendents are deeply involved in establishing the principal selection process, but often wait to interview until the committee identifies two or three top candidates. According to the Baltzell and Dentler (1983) study, superintendents in exemplary districts delay involvement until the final moment in order to avoid any appearance of undue influence. If the perception gets out that it's a Good Old Person process, it's all over—you may as well get another superintendent.

Training the Interview Team

Involving a broad base of people in the screening and selection process may be counterproductive unless district personnel train those individuals in legal guidelines and multiple assessment techniques. A personnel director with whom I spoke said he conducts a four-hour training session with the screening and interview committee. Incorporated into this session are discussions of various laws that govern the selection process, such as "protected classes" of candidates, interviewing techniques, appropriate and inappropriate questions, and formulation of interview questions and procedures by the committee. Without such training, interviewers' choices may be unduly influenced by factors such as attitude congruence, first impressions, and personal biases.

Structuring the Interview

The reliability of the interview process is strengthened when the interview is structured, when candidates are asked identical, predetermined, well-formulated questions. In addition, effective interviews include simulations, written exercises, and situational questions. This contrasts with the practice of those districts that conduct interviews in a causal manner, actually allowing candidates to control the flow of the interview.

A key element in districts that employ exemplary interview practices is the use of a set of situational questions that require candidates to respond to actual school problems, such as the following:

1. As a principal, you face a student who has been sent to the office for making an obscene gesture to a teacher. The student reports that the teacher has on more than one occasion called him a "jerk" in front of the class. What are the issues and what will you do?

2. The district has a practice that athletic teams playing in a state championship late night game may come to school two hours late the following morning. The District also requires band and rally to attend the game. You are approached by members of the rally squad and band who want the same consideration as that given the team because they are required to be in attendance. How will you respond?

3. You're the only administrator in the building. A parent bursts into your office and in loud, derisive language complains that a teacher has dealt unfairly with his child. The parent has a long list of complaints but focuses primarily on a recent classroom confrontation. The student has a reputation for being a troublemaker. How will you deal with the parent?

Performance simulations are another useful part of the interview process. In simulations, applicants demonstrate certain skills for interviewers. In one district that incorporates simulation exercises in the interview process, each candidate views a twenty-minute classroom lesson designed specifically for the interview simulation by a staff development teacher. The candidate then prepares an observation report and holds a conference with the staff development teacher who taught the lesson. A committee member observes this conference. Finally, the staff development teacher rates each candidate's conferencing and observation skills.

Written simulations on situational or inbasket problems are other exercises that districts can use.

Other Sources of Information

It is crucial for the interview team to consider both the information gathered in the interview and the information gathered from other sources, such as applications, transcripts, teaching and administrative performance, references, and assessment center data. If the finalists are not from within the system, districts should also conduct site visits in finalists' schools and communities to inquire about the candidates' qualifications. If the hiring decision is based solely on a thirty- to sixty-minute interview, chances are high that the best candidate may be overlooked.

In sum, exemplary districts use a comprehensive system to screen and select capable principals. They adopt written selection policies, develop specific selection criteria, identify the specific opening in vacancy announcements, involve and train a broad base of people in screening and selection, use multiple means of assessment, and consider varied sources of information about candidates.

Recommendations for Recruiting and Selecting

1. Develop written policies. As a beginning, school boards need to develop written policies that declare the district's commitment to hiring the most capable principals. Before the board can decide upon a selection process, its members must first agree on their aims. What kind of schools do they want to foster? What kind of administrators are they looking for?

Once board members have agreed upon goals, they can decide the specific criteria to be used when the district starts looking for a principal. To that end, the board should require an intensive job analysis prior to hiring.

2. Create a pool of qualified candidates. Long before specific vacancies arise, the district should identify a pool of potential leaders and develop a "pipeline" to the principalship. Such a system can provide the developmental experiences that will qualify members of the pool to be principals. District training programs, internships, and the assignment of teachers to various leadership roles are various ways of grooming a cadre of capable candidates. Better yet, a training and internship program that welcomes women and minority candidates may offset any disadvantages for these groups.

3. Develop specific selection criteria. It is essential that selectors, before announcing a vacancy, develop specific criteria-based standards that encompass all the duties and skills required in the principalship. Selectors should consider and solicit, formally or informally, the opinions of teachers, parents, students, and other administrators concerning the kind of principal they want and need.

Even technically sound selection processes will fail if school officials have not honestly examined their own visions for the school, their aims in selecting candidates, and the kind of evidence to be gathered for use in appraising candidates on the basis of stated criteria.

4. Identify the specific opening in vacancy announcements. Although districts often hire principals to serve in different schools during their years of service, it is advantageous to identify in the vacancy announcement the particular school where the opening exists. Knowing the specific needs and characteristics of a school can help the new principal prepare for a successful experience and can help selectors identify the best principal for that particular position. Vacancy announcements should include pertinent information about the school, such as composition of staff and students, community characteristics, and so forth. In addition, the announcements should list the skills, traits, and experience necessary for a candidate to successfully compete for the position.

5. Recruit widely. School districts should not only train indistrict staff for future principalships, they should also recruit aggressively outside the district. "New blood" is one benefit and finding the best candidate is another. Advertising widely in college job placement bulletins and professional organizations' newsletters is one method of attracting applicants from a wider geographic area. Targeting talented individuals in other districts and helping them establish an entry to the district's network is another recruitment strategy. Districts enhance their ability to find the best candidates when they seek out a large number of applicants.

6. Involve a broad base of people in screening and selection. Use of selection teams increases the reliability of interviews by combining the judgments and perceptions of a variety of individuals. The inclusion of school-based administrators, teachers, and parents can guard against the "groupthink" mentality that may be present in small, cohesive groups of central office administrators.

7. Train those who select principals. Selecting a capable principal is a difficult yet essential task. Involving a broad base of people in the screening and selection process requires that districts train those individuals in legal guidelines and multiple assessment techniques. Without such training, interviewers' choices may be unduly influenced by factors such as attitude congruence, first impressions, biases, and a notion of "fit" rather than "merit."

8. Use multiple means of assessment. Districts should use a combination of strategies to screen and select principals. Although the district can design an effective interview, assessment center data, written simulations, clinical simulations, and situational questions should also be part of districts' selection processes. These techniques increase districts' chances of selecting principals on the basis of merit and skill.

9. Consider varied sources of information about candidates. In addition to simulations that give districts samples of candidates' skills, it is advisable to collect information from other sources as well. Site visits, references, academic records, placement file recommendations, and written statements of philosophy are other types of information that districts should consider.

Finding the most capable principal doesn't end with selection. Although the search for a principal ends when he or she is hired, the process is far from over. Selecting good leaders is only half the battle; the other half is helping them succeed and grow in the job. Well- organized postselection activities including orientations, professional development activities, opportunities for networking, and on-the-job assistance from experienced administrators are likely to help newly hired principals succeed. The next chapter looks at the important task of inducting beginning principals into their new leadership positions.

PRINCIPALS

HOW TO TRAIN, RECRUIT, SELECT, **INDUCT,** AND EVALUATE LEADERS FOR AMERICA'S SCHOOLS

INDUCTING PRINCIPALS

> Entry is a quintessential situation, when the "hopes and fears of all the years" are again rekindled—when the dreams and visions of both the person entering and the organization inviting are arouse—when all the anxieties of facing the unknown are at their highest pitch—when one experiences the ritual of initiation into the mysteries of this particular tribe. (Tobert 1982)

Each year nearly eleven thousand individuals enter a school in the United States as the new principal (Pharis and Zakariya 1979). The vast majority of these beginning principals experience two distinct emotions upon entry: excitement at having been selected for one of the most critical positions in America's schools, and anxiety about their ability to meet the demands of the job (Sosne 1982).

Unfortunately, many first-year principals experience a "sink-or-swim, learn-on-your-own" induction to the job that, in turn, increases their anxiety about fulfilling their responsibilities. Roland Barth (1980) contends that a new principal often gets "a title, an office, responsibility, accountability, and obligations. Nothing more." Barth writes that when a new principal begins work, school officials often say, "You were hired for the school because, among the hundreds of qualified applicants, we felt you could do the job. Now do it."

School officials' nonchalance concerning their new principals' needs is badly misguided, Daniel Duke (1987) suggests. "The first days and months of the principalship are critical to the process of shaping school leaders," and what happens during an individual's first year as principal may exert "a major influence on his or her subsequent performance." Research also suggests that early experiences during the induction period to a new organizational setting and position can strongly affect employee attitudes, skills, behaviors, and performance.

Meryl Reis Louis (1980) points out that the first six to ten months in a new job is a crucial "transition period" in which newcomers need information and assistance from veteran members of the organization. This period is one in which neophytes are most receptive to assistance and to learning new skills. Thus, the entry-year experiences of principals and the processes that school district's use to induct beginning principals may have a profound impact on their skill development, attitudes, actions, and effectiveness.

Given the importance of a principal's leadership and the potential influence of the induction year on rookie administrators, it is clear that school districts must begin addressing the needs of beginning principals, enabling them to lead rather than merely survive. This chapter begins by describing the needs of beginning principals and the problems they encounter due, in part, to poor induction practices. Next, promising induction strategies are highlighted, followed by induction recommendations that school districts may utilize to assist rookies in adjusting to the role of school leader. The chapter concludes with a checklist new principals may use to make their first year on the job more successful.

Experiences of Beginning Principals: The Problems

"This job isn't at all what I expected." Such statements, or unspoken thoughts, are common among newly hired individuals. Everett Hughes (1958) has likened the plight of newcomers to a form of "reality shock," where individuals experience "surprises" that arise from differences between their "anticipatory socialization"—what they thought or were told the job would be like—and their actual experiences in the new setting.

Based on principals' comments about their first year on the job, it appears that the "shock of entry" is common among rookie administrators. When left on their own, many experience problems that inhibit their ability to provide the kind of leadership needed for school excellence. With this in mind, what are the surprises, frustrations, needs, and problems that new principals face and how can school districts provide assistance for these fledgling administrators to help ensure their success?

Isolation

For many, the extreme isolation of the principalship comes as a shock. After some brief orientations, many districts simply give newly hired principals the keys to the building and, in effect, say "sink or swim, you're on your own." Isolated and without guidance, newcomers often make mistakes that may have long-term consequences.

Many rookies in my study of beginning principals in Oregon and Washington felt isolated and found the position to be a lonely one. The learn-on-your-own induction system employed by many districts exacerbates a major problem of the principalship: physical isolation from colleagues. As one principal said, "This has got to be one of the loneliest jobs because when I was a v.p. you could go in and talk to the principal about a problem, you have someone to share it with. You just don't have it here [in the principal's chair]." The fact that many decisions rest on the principal's shoulders also contributed to the sense of isolation. Another principal noted, "The buck stops in my office. It's the old decision business. I'm it."

In a study of beginning administrators, Robert Nelson (1986) also found a sense of isolation among newcomers. Although some administrators had previously worked in collaborative environments, there was "little opportunity to collaborate in their new position." Others, while not having come from a collaborative environment, told Nelson they "looked to administration as providing the autonomy to seek out collaborative opportunities with other administrators." Unfortunately, they found little opportunity to work with colleagues.

In his study, Daresh (1987b) documented similar feelings of isolation and lack of collegial support among principals in the Midwest. He recommends that "ways need to be found to ensure that, whenever possible, new administrators are not left totally alone to solve problems in isolation from their colleagues." One reason it is important to address the issue of isolation is that it, in turn, contributes to many other problems that newcomers experience.

Time Management

A second major problem and source of surprise that many beginning principals experience is dealing with details and numerous demands inherent in the principalship that, in turn, cause time management problems. Marrion (1983), in her study of beginning principals in Colorado, discovered that "time management" was beginning principals' "number one problem." She concluded that beginning principals need to know which tasks to delegate and to whom, and "they need to know how to assign priorities to tasks, manage the myriad of details that are part of the principalship, and arrange their time so that they can be pro-active as opposed to re-active."

A 1987 study of beginning principals conducted by the Kentucky Association of School Administrators and the Appalachian Education Laboratory (KASA-AEL) also found that the most frequent recommendation made by new principals regarding inservice needs was in the area of time management. Nearly 62 percent of the first-year principals who participated in the study mentioned time management as a need. And many beginning principals in my study stated that the time pressure and the time commitment of a principal's job were overwhelming. One principal commented: "There just doesn't seem to be enough time. I didn't anticipate the day would be so fragmented. This job is so demanding and I feel pulled from all directions."

During the induction period, school districts should provide assistance to new principals about ways to handle administrative details. New principals would then have more time to focus energy on instructional leadership issues and would feel less overwhelmed. The principals in Marrion's study recommended that "school districts organize a new-principal orientation which would provide information regarding district-specific tasks, procedures for completing those tasks, and a calendar which notes the due dates of those tasks." Interestingly, the principals studied were also unanimous in their belief that time-management training would be more effective after they are familiar with the demands of the job. Consequently, they wanted such inservice during their first year on the job rather than during preservice preparation.

Technical Problems

Learning the technical aspects of the job is a third major problem facing new principals. Beginning administrators report a variety of concerns in the technical or procedural area. Learning the "logistics" of many mundane, yet important, school system-specific procedures consumes a lot of beginning principals' time. For example, new principals must grapple with such concerns as how to interpret computer printouts from the district business office; how to set up for assemblies and lunch; how to address various legal issues; and how to operate the bells, clocks, and firebells. One principal recalls,

> Standing in the office on Labor Day looking at the clock
> and wondering, "How in the hell do you ring the bell?"
> is perhaps my most vivid memory. It also sums up
> many of the things I encountered that were simple but
> were things I had not done before. (Duke 1987)

After completing his study of beginning principals in the Midwest, Daresh wrote, "If any one single area of beginning administrator concerns could be classified as most powerful, this area of perceived lack of technical expertise related to how to follow established procedures was it." Because they receive little assistance in this area, many newcomers spend considerable time learning technical procedures unrelated to leadership but essential for the smooth operation of a school.

Elizabeth DuBose (1986) surveyed eighty principals in South Carolina concerning the task-specific assistance and information needs of incoming elementary school principals. She discovered that principals, upon entering a new district, had a vital need for information in the technical area, but the information and assistance provided was far "less than the extent to which the needs were expressed by principals." The KASA-AEL study also found that beginning principals spent the majority of their time seeking assistance with such tasks as "completing reports, dealing with budgets, working to figure out the system."

In my research of 167 rookies in the Northwest, learning building-level budgeting, supervision of accounting and purchasing procedures, and details related to the opening and closing of school were technical aspects of the job for which beginners reported a vital need for information and assistance. Many of the principals, however, received limited guidance when struggling to learn these unfamiliar tasks. One principal captures the frustration of learning technical aspects of the job:

> When it came time to do budgeting, I opened that sucker
> up [the budget printout] and looked at all that stuff. It

was like Greek. I didn't have a clue, not a clue, as to where to start. You talk about codes. It is written in code, and I had to take a great deal of time just to learn how to decipher it.

As Louis suggests, a learn-on-your-own philosophy of orientation can be quite dysfunctional. In many other occupations, the learning process occurs more gradually. For example, as Dan Lortie (1975) points out, "Business, building crafts, and highly skilled trades require formal apprenticeships where the neophyte is ushered through a series of tasks of ascending difficulty and assumes greater responsibility as his technical competence increases." Yet it appears that many neophyte principals must quickly scale a very steep learning curve with little help.

Socialization to the School System

A fourth major area of concern for new principals is "how to get things done." As Louis points out, learning "how we do things around here" is part of the culture-content information that newcomers need to learn during the transition period to function effectively within an organization. Beginning administrators in Nelson's study reported they were eventually able to learn the "logistics"; however, far more difficult to grasp "were the strategies which the organization regarded as appropriate to the roles they assumed and the social relations in the organization."

Beginning principals in Daresh's study experienced similar socialization problems. For example, one principal told Daresh he felt foolish after following procedures outlined in the school board policy manual regarding requests for new equipment. Stated policy required the principal to file an application with the assistant superintendent in charge of administrative services. After failing to receive response to the equipment request form, he learned that it wasn't customary to follow procedures in this area. Instead of bothering the assistant superintendent who, after all, was too busy dealing with matters that were not listed as his responsibility in the policy manual, the principal dealt directly with the director of buildings and grounds. Daresh says:

> The new principal discovered this discrepancy between stated policy and real procedure only after talking to another, more experienced principal who noted that the request for equipment would probably only gather dust

"in somebody's in-basket" and would never be acted upon if "normal channels" were followed.

Information about "unwritten" rules, procedures, and expectations was considered one of the most important areas for assistance among new principals in my study. Learning the unwritten modes of operation within districts was necessary for new principals to get things done. Furthermore, such information was vital for guiding principals' actions and for understanding what district officials expected of the principal. The principals I interviewed stated with considerable emotion the tremendous time and energy they had to exert, often by trial and error, to learn subtle, district-specific nuances.

"Learning the ropes," political and social, of a particular district can be difficult for newly hired principals. Many important pieces of information about school system operations are unwritten, and rookies must depend on others to transmit this information to them. Some unwritten rules can be gleaned by observing experienced principals. Unfortunately, beginners often are unable to observe veterans because they are physically isolated from other administrators or they do not believe they are good role models.

Communication with other principals is another way beginners can obtain needed information, but Nelson found that districts in his study did not facilitate interaction among administrators. Left on their own and not wanting to appear incompetent in the eyes of more experienced colleagues, some newcomers sought advice from individuals outside the school system. Nelson found that this approach "did not present the organization-specific information that the newcomers sought."

In her study, DuBose also documented the problems that incoming principals had in obtaining needed information and assistance from veterans. To address principals' information and assistance needs, DuBose recommends the following:

1. School districts should recognize the importance of the transition period for incoming principals and implement a plan by which the needed assistance and information can be provided in a thorough and systematic manner.

2. The immediate supervisor of an incoming principal and the outgoing principal of a school should recognize their

responsibility for providing the needed assistance and information during the transition period and should work in concert with the district to structure appropriate entry experiences.

Lack of Feedback

A final area of concern among beginning principals is lack of feedback. M. London (1985) suggests that feedback about performance and discussions of organizational mission have a significant impact on neophytes' commitment to the system and on their loyalty to the goals and values of the organization. Constructive, specific feedback can also help newcomers improve their knowledge about the principal's role and their leadership skills and actions.

Performance evaluations by superiors can provide feedback and guidance to newly hired principals. Unfortunately, many beginners report such performance feedback is infrequent and not specific or helpful. Nelson found that most beginning administrators he interviewed "wished that they received more specific feedback from their superiors about their job performance. But formal feedback was rarely given."

Daresh reports similar concerns among beginning principals with whom he spoke.

> They never knew if they were really doing what was considered to be a good job, and no one in their schools or districts appeared inclined to provide much feedback or direction to help them understand how they were doing. This lack of feedback was an issue that principals felt from every level of the organization—superiors, peers, and subordinates. (1987b)

Over half of the principals I studied reported inadequate feedback on their performance as a characteristic of school district induction practices that made their first year more difficult. Without feedback from superiors, new principals were anxious, tentative, indecisive, and uneasy about their performance. They coped with a lack of feedback from superiors by relying on informal comments from staff and students to get a reading on their performance and where they needed to improve.

It is clear that beginning principals' performance may be improved with specific feedback, encouragement, and guidance from successful and experienced administrators in or outside of a school system. As we will see in chapter 4, lack of feedback on performance is also a concern of veteran principals.

Other Needs of the New Principal

Much research on the needs of beginning principals is still "unseasoned," merely in its beginning stages. Although the issue of principal preservice training has recently received increased attention from policymakers and educators, Daresh notes that few studies of the needs of beginning principals "have been carried out during the past few years."

The purpose of my research on the needs of beginning principals in Oregon and Washington was, in part, to begin filling that gap in the research (Anderson 1989b). Drawing generalizations from the Oregon-Washington sample to other areas of the country should be done cautiously. With this in mind, the study's findings do provide an indication of the tasks for which beginners need assistance. Table 1 lists twenty-one administrative tasks, rank ordered by need, that new principals reported as areas where the greatest need for help exists.

These twenty-one administrative tasks were distributed under the categories of Organization and Structure, Staff Personnel, Instructional and Curriculum Development, and School Finance and Business Management. Principals also reported *some* need for assistance and information in the areas of School-Community Relations and School Facilities. Finally, principals generally agreed on tasks for which little or no assistance was needed. Those tasks were in the areas of School Transportation, Food Services, and Student Personnel.

The beginning principals in my study reported that they needed more assistance and information for working with and leading adults than for working with and leading students. Many principals in the study were unprepared for or surprised by the challenge of working with and resolving conflicts among adults, whereas they found their interactions with students were a source of satisfaction. This is not surprising given the fact that many new principals have spent the majority of their careers working with and leading young people, not adults. As one principal noted, "Although I enjoy working with adults, it has been a frustrating and challenging learning experience."

TABLE 1. Administrative Tasks on Which Beginning Principals Had a Vital or Important Need for Assistance and Information

Task	Rank
Plan and manage school budget	1
Understand "unwritten" rules, procedures, and expectations	2
Plan and direct improvements in curriculum and instruction	3
Understand district goals, philosophy, and expectations of principals	4
Orientation to and understanding of staff	5
Assess relevance of instruction, curriculum, and evaluate program outcomes	6
Understand and implement school board policies, district rules, and administrative procedures	7
Supervise accounting procedures for school monies	8
Understand curriculum content, objectives, and organization	9
Understand and work through district decision making processes	10
Assess community needs, problems, and expectations	11
Develop master schedule	12
Set goals and develop long-range plans	13
Supervise and evaluate staff	14
Deal with staff concerns and resolve conflicts	15
Help staff improve and plan staff development activities	16
Select, assign, and orient staff	17
Supervise and direct custodial services, maintenance of facilities, and plant systems	18
Supervise special programs	19
Supervise purchasing procedures	20
Coordinate the opening and closing of each school year	21

Beginners cited lack of experience and inadequate preservice training in three areas—leading the instructional program, planning and managing the building budget, and supervising and evaluating staff—as reasons why they had a high need for help in these areas. And, as noted previously, understanding the unwritten rules and expectations in a district was one area in which new principals wanted and needed a great deal of assistance.

Considering the problems of isolation, time management, lack of technical guidance and orientation to the school culture, and inadequate feedback on performance, what training activities might help new principals to lead their schools?

Promising Induction Programs

As many principals report, preservice training never fully prepared them for the realities of the principalship. Most of their learning occurs on the job, and learning how to be effective, especially without help or guidance, can be painful and frustrating. In an analysis of principals' work, Kent Peterson (1985) proposes several factors that may hinder principals' on-the-job learning:

1. Principals' preference for action in solving problems works against reflective self-assessment and learning.

2. Infrequent formal opportunities to share experiences with colleagues inhibit peer learning and prevent principals from capitalizing on a store-house of experience.

3. Professional growth and measurement of progress are hindered by feedback from superiors that is non-specific and abstract.

According to Stanley Schainker and LaRaine Roberts (1987), "What emerges from practice and research is paradoxical: principals' most valuable source of learning is their on-the-job experience, yet the reality of that experience is seriously limited as a vehicle for learning." It is clear that beginning principals need a structured, systematic process for learning how to deal effectively with various school-specific problems. Educators are beginning to recognize that school districts cannot afford to leave beginning principals alone—isolated from helpful colleagues—to solve complex problems. Thus, several institutions have begun development of promising programs that can assist beginning principals.

Peer-Assisted Leadership

During fall 1983, the Far West Laboratory for Educational Research and Development began Peer-Assisted Leadership (PAL), a unique professional development activity that allows school principals to analyze their own leadership behavior and that of a peer partner in a nonprescriptive, nonjudgmental manner. During a year-long process, principals learn and apply various skills for collecting data about their partners and sharing that information with them in a useful way.

Bruce Barnett (1985) describes PAL training as consisting of a series of six full-day meetings occurring at six-week at intervals. During these meetings, trainers from the Instructional Management Program of the Far West Lab instruct participants in various skills for gathering and analyzing information. These include shadowing techniques to observe their peer partner, reflective interviewing, advanced reflective interviewing and theme building, clustering data by themes, final model production, and model presentations. Between meetings, Barnett reports, principals apply the skills by conducting observations and interviews that provide data about their partners' schools. During the final meeting, principals are prepared to present models of their partners' instructional management activities to the whole group.

As a result of the PAL process, participants say they benefit from working with other principals and engage in more self-reflection, a process useful in running their schools. Principals also report that they receive many new and helpful suggestions from their partners about how to handle particular problems.

Since PAL's inception, several districts have involved principals in the program. Ginny Lee, PAL trainer, states that the San Diego School District has used the program as part of its induction program for beginning principals. In San Diego, senior administrators are paired with rookies, and the partners implement PAL techniques in assisting each other on school-specific leadership concerns.

Two new principals I interviewed, who participated in the PAL process through the Northwest Regional Educational Laboratory, believed pairing principals from different districts was very beneficial. As one noted, "I could share anything with my partner, and I knew it was safe. I wouldn't always take that kind of risk in my own district." Thus, being paired with someone removed from the district in which the principal works may create a safer environment for nonjudgmental feedback.

Ginny Lee (1988) reports that the Far West Lab has developed a training-of-trainers component to the program to increase the number of administrators who can participate. Bruce Barnett and Faye Mueller (1987), in a study of the long-term effects of the PAL training on principals, found that collegial observation and reflective feedback have enduring, positive effects on participating principals. PAL also produced a significant, indirect benefit for the two principals I interviewed: the program fostered a professional relationship between these newcomers that will continue for many years.

If nothing else, perhaps the most important benefits for new principals who participate in collegial feedback programs such as PAL are that they may be more interested in continually improving their leadership efforts, more willing to engage in reflective activities, and more open to feedback about their leadership performance. Furthermore, structured opportunities for greater collegial support can help address many of the problems, frustrations, and concerns of beginning principals, particularly isolation and lack of feedback.

Principals Inservice Program

Another program with an emphasis on collegial support is the Principals Inservice Program developed in 1979 by the Institute for Development of Educational Activities (I/D/E/A/). James LaPlant (1979), director of the project, suggests that most

> inservice education for principals can be characterized as a smorgasbord of opportunities splattered on the schoolhouse wall in a way which leaves principals trying to decide if the wall is part of a large mural, a piece of abstract art, or perhaps an unwanted act of vandalism.

Avoiding the practice of exposing principals to a "bag of tricks" in a one-shot inservice session, I/D/E/A/ developed its program to assist principals by establishing "long-term" collegial support groups to provide school-specific improvement. These

61

groups, each headed by an I/D/E/A/-trained facilitator, are usually composed of six to ten principals who meet monthly over a two-year period.

The goal of the program is to help principals improve their ability to lead school programs that will help children learn. To that end, principals meet as a group to explore problems in their schools that demand solutions. LaPlant states, "In a climate of openness, trust, and mutual assistance, principals become resources for ideas and peer reviews in the professional development and school improvement efforts." Outcomes of the program typically fall in four categories:

- *Personal Professional Development.* The principal, as a member of a collegial support group, designs, implements, and evaluates a personal professional development plan to increase his or her leadership capability.

- *School Improvement.* The principal, as a member of a collegial support group, designs, implements, and evaluates a school improvement project to address an identified need within the school.

- *Collegial Support Group.* Members of the collegial support group provide assistance and encouragement to one another as they engage in their professional development and school improvement efforts.

- *Continuous Improvement.* The principal accepts responsibility for the achievement of personal professional development and school improvement goals.

In a study of participants in the I/D/E/A/ program, Daresh (1982) concluded that collegial support has a tremendous potential for improving the quality of inservice support available to school principals:

> Particularly for beginning principals, the collegial support group concept allows administrators to work cooperatively to propose solutions for numerous daily problems and, even more important, to escape from the need to devote all their time and energy to daily managerial issues and tasks. Thus, principals are free to exercise a more creative approach to problem solving and may, over time, engage in the often illusive role of instructional leaders of their schools.

The I/D/E/A/ program has become very popular among principals. According to Karen Fearing, administrative assistant at I/D/E/A/, since its inception in 1978, the Principals Inservice Program has grown rapidly. Today, it includes three hundred facilitators leading collegial support groups involving more than three thousand principals in twenty-eight states and three foreign countries.

Although collegial programs like those developed by Far West Lab and I/D/E/A/ can play an important role in assisting beginners, individual school districts must also take an active role in the process by providing beginning principals with a variety of well planned, helpful induction activities. Joseph Rogus and William Drury (1988) have designed a framework for school districts to use in developing a principal induction plan.

Model of Principal Induction

According to Rogus and Drury, their induction model is one that will improve "first-year administrator performance, increase the retention rate of beginning administrators, and develop an 'esprit de corps' among administrative staff." Specific program goals are listed in table 2.

TABLE 2. Induction Program Purposes

Induction program participants will be able to:

1. Demonstrate understanding of system expectations, procedures, and resources.

2. Demonstrate increased competence and comfort in addressing building or unit outcomes or concerns.

3. Enhance their personal/professional growth.

4. Develop a personal support system.

5. Receive personalized assistance in coping with building/unit problems.

6. Receive formative feedback and assistance toward strengthening their administrative performance.

Source: Rogus and Drury (1988)

TABLE 3. Program Structure and Essential Program Elements

Large Group	Small Group	Mentoring
1. Presentation with respect to content/process needs identified by program participants (2)	2. Group support sessions with a problem-solving emphasis (4)	1. Individual helping relationships to building/concerns (5)
2. Presentations with respect to system expectations, procedures, and resources (1)	2. Group support for implementing plan (3.4)	2. Provision of formative feedback on administrative performance (6)
3. Development of personal/professional growth plans (3)		3. Individual support for implementing personal growth plan (3)

Note: Numbers in parentheses signify the program goals (listed in table 2) to which program elements are keyed.

Source: Rogus and Drury (1988)

To achieve these goals, Rogus and Drury developed three components for implementing an induction program: large-group, small-group, and mentoring. Table 3 shows how these three essential components help participants achieve the six goals of the authors' induction model.

The Large-Group Component. Activities in the large-group setting are designed to focus on the concerns, problems, and issues that district staff and administrative participants identify. Rogus and Drury state, "While it is important that participants understand the expectations of the district, it is equally important that they receive help on the issues and concerns that they view as significant." They also say that the large group can serve as an effective setting for development of professional growth plans.

The Small-Group Component. Small groups serve as a vehicle for providing individual assistance with implementation of the personal growth plans. A district can also use this group to help beginning principals address building or unit problems, similar to the collegial support groups in the /I/D/E/A/ program. Rogus and Drury note that "each small group is composed of five or six administrators in similar job positions. Members of the group divide into pairs and share growth outcomes and action steps on a regular basis.

The Mentoring Component. In this part of the induction program, veteran administrators are paired with beginners in a "buddy system." According to Rogus and Drury, "mentors tend to be effective if they choose to serve as mentors, are effective in their work, are recognized as being successful, and are trained for the role." Because of the complexity of the mentoring relationship, Rogus and Drury advise that senior officials carefully match mentors and beginners.

Mentors meet with their partners on a regular basis to provide support and assistance. They provide assistance to the beginner in carrying out a personal growth plan, providing feedback on administrative performance, and helping the rookie principal focus not only on immediate concerns, but also on questions that "transcend the urgencies which normally dominate a first-year principal's thinking." In a sense, Rogus and Drury write, "the mentor's task is to help the mentee... develop a clear vision of what the organization might become" and to reflect on the mentee's leadership actions.

The three-pronged principal induction model that Rogus and Drury designed serves as a framework for communicating the expectations of the district to new principals. As the authors suggest, it can encourage support among status equals:

> It allows for clinical support, coaching, and corrective
> feedback by practitioners; and it diffuses responsibility
> for providing corrective feedback, training, and support.
> The programs can also serve as a helpful mechanism for
> recruiting and selecting new members.

Although the induction system that Rogus and Drury offer provides a model school systems can use to induct principals, many districts may not have a large enough pool of principals to create such peer interactions. Thus, cooperative arrangements between districts or with universities may provide another means of assisting beginning principals with relevant induction support.

Universities and Professional Associations
Assist Beginning Principals

Joseph Licata and Chad Ellett (1988) believe universities can and should play a role in assisting school districts induct beginning principals. They argue, "University professors, school districts, and other professional associations all have a stake in the professional success of new school administrators and can work together in providing successful induction experiences." In Louisiana, Licata and Ellett report, five state universities and several school districts are working together to provide beginning principals with a "clinical induction system."

The Louisiana induction system begins with a comprehensive diagnostic assessment of each participating principal's professional performance and work environment. Then, through a series of seminars, trainers help principals analyze results, solve problems, and develop action plans on site- specific issues. Trainers also identify common needs based on assessment profiles, and they provide technical assistance in coordinating presenters for seminars throughout the year. As Licata and Ellett note, the "delivery system and induction program capitalizes on new principals' first work context as a means for providing a more job relevant set of instructional activities."

Professional associations can also play an important role in helping new principals succeed by exposing newcomers to savvy and successful veteran principals and helping them identify the right questions to ask during their first year. In Washington State, leaders and veteran principals in the Association of Washington School Principals (AWSP) organize a two-day summer conference for new principals preceding their first year on the job. Areas covered during the AWSP conference include:

- How to succeed as a first-year principal

- How to work with and support the school district's superintendent

- How to develop a successful relationship with the central office

- How to formulate an administrative plan for positive staff evaluation

- How to emphasize positive aspects of the building budget

- How to be successful in relationships with parents

- How to develop a process for dealing with emergencies, tragedies, and legal concerns

- How to separate who you are from what you do

According to an AWSP bulletin (1988), the response of participants can be summed up by a comment expressed on one of the conference evaluations: "Great job! The information was just what I needed to get started on the right foot."

A similar conference for newcomers—based on the KASA-AEL study group's investigation of beginning principals' needs—is held in Kentucky. In addition, a principal advocacy program sponsored by the Confederation of Oregon School Administrators (COSA) is another example of a strategy professional associations can use to assist new principals. In the COSA program, new principals are paired with veteran principals to whom they can turn for help during their first year in the principalship.

Although universities and professional associations can assist newcomers, it is naive to believe that out-of-district inservice programs will provide aspiring administrators with all they need to know about being an effective leader in a particular school district. School districts, therefore, assume primary responsibility for providing newly hired principals with a variety of supportive induction activities to help them succeed and grow as school leaders.

Recommendations for Induction: The School District's Role

Too often, principals are tossed into the job without sufficient support from their superiors. Some, in fact, find that their performance is judged according to how little they bother the central office. Good superintendents, however, ensure that new principals are aware of the values, beliefs, and norms of the communities where they are assigned, and that they share the district's or supervisory body's aims and goals. Effective superiors, therefore, provide the guidance and technical support from experienced peers that will help new principals adjust and succeed. (U.S. Department of Education 1987)

Although the search for a principal ends when the person is hired, the process of getting an outstanding principal is far from over. Developing a well-thought-out process for inducting principals into their new leadership role is, therefore, an activity that hiring officials cannot afford to ignore. Rather, it should be considered a high priority. To help guide school districts' principal induction efforts, the following recommendations are provided to address needs and problems of new principals.

1. Orient beginning principals to the district. Districts should provide newly hired principals with a comprehensive orientation to the district. This starts with the selection process, when hiring officials should provide applicants with a clear understanding of the district, community, and supervisory body's goals and aims, as well as any unusual challenges that a new principal may face when beginning work. Next, scheduled orientations with important school system offices, such as business, transportation, maintenance, public relations, and curriculum, should be included as part of a comprehensive orientation program that is spread out over a new principal's first year on the job.

The purpose of initial orientations should be to familiarize the new principal with the persons who can answer questions as issues arise; they should not inundate beginning principals with unnecessary new information. In small school districts, orientation responsibility may fall upon the superintendent. In larger systems, orientations are often coordinated by a team of senior administrators.

2. Orient beginning principals to their schools. The outgoing principal has a professional responsibility to provide needed assistance and information to a beginning principal and should work in concert with the district office to develop a plan for the new principal's entry experiences. Ideally, outgoing principals need to provide their replacements with specific information about building schedules and procedures, staff strengths and weaknesses, and local community leaders' and parents' expectations. If the previous principal is not available for this type of site-specific orientation, district office supervisors and other principals in the district should provide the needed assistance and information.

3. Institute a buddy system. School districts should pair successful veteran principals with rookies in a "buddy system" to help newcomers learn the "informal ropes" of a district. For outside appointees, assignment of a veteran will probably be necessary, but for inside candidates, hiring officials and the newcomers themselves should confer about who might be the best match for them. The veteran principal should provide technical and cultural-specific information and assistance, giving the new principal insight into the subtle signs, signals, and norms of the district.

A buddy or "mentor" principal system should be instituted with caution. Unless they are carefully chosen and trained, mentor principals may squelch creative innovations and new ideas of beginning principals. Untrained mentors may simply pass on ineffective practices, perpetuating traditional processes and norms that may need to change. Effective mentors, therefore, must not tell beginning principals what to do, but should guide newcomers so they are able to make their own decisions based on a thorough understanding of the potential consequences of their choices. As Daresh suggests, "Mentors who would try to make inexperienced principals behave as they would are probably not mentors at all."

Finding effective mentors may be difficult, especially for small districts. Smaller school systems may need to reach out to other districts to secure effective mentors. Educational service districts and professional associations may also need to facilitate cooperative mentor-mentee programs for districts not large enough to develop their own.

4. Structure beginners' workload. Beginning principals need to spend a great deal of time in their buildings to develop productive working relationships with staff, students, and parents and to assess various aspects of their schools' programs and operations. Hence, senior administrators must protect beginners from activities that divert energy away from learning about their school. For example, districts should not involve newly hired principals in a variety of district projects and committees. This only complicates the task of learning the system. Veteran principals often complain about being pulled out of their buildings to attend meetings called by the district office; for newcomers, such a practice can be even more disruptive.

5. *Give beginning principals feedback.* Districts should develop a system whereby beginning principals are provided with specific, constructive feedback about their performance. Principals' supervisors should provide both formal and informal feedback throughout the year. Because superiors may be judgmental in their assessments and are often deeply involved in other district responsibilities, many educators recommend a collegial supervisory model, such as Peer-Assisted Leadership and Principals Inservice Program, to provide principals with feedback. Regardless, a well- designed performance feedback system is needed to counteract the tentativeness that appears to result from current practice.

6. *Develop a plan for professional growth.* If beginning principals are to continue to develop leadership skills and grow professionally, districts must assess newcomers' general leadership strengths and weaknesses as well as their skills and knowledge regarding district-specific priorities. Such assessments can be as formal as the NASSP assessment center simulations or can be tailored to fit each particular district's needs. Superiors, colleagues, and beginners should all be involved in assessing a newcomer's needs and then help the beginner develop a growth plan that includes specific learning objectives, activities to help in the development process, an implementation timeline, and an evaluation plan.

7. *Facilitate peer-group problem solving and idea sharing.* Districts should bring together beginning principals and innovative practitioners in idea- sharing and problem-solving sessions to discuss beginners' experiences, offer suggestions for handling specific problems, share ideas for building- specific issues, and expose newcomers to innovative practices. Districts that do not have enough beginning principals to create such peer interaction should enter into cooperative arrangements with other districts. Again, state professional associations, educational service districts, and even universities can assist in coordinating seminars that bring beginning principals together for supportive, reflective discussions.

8. *Facilitate regional inservice.* Districts, universities, professional associations, and other educational training institutes need to facilitate regional inservice opportunities for principals in areas of budget planning and management, teacher supervision and evaluation, time management and conflict management, and leading instructional and curricular improvement efforts. Such inservice sessions should bring together experienced principals and beginners to share ideas.

An Entry-Year Checklist for Beginning Principals

In addition to the above list of induction strategies school districts can adopt to help new principals succeed, there are also some practical steps that rookies themselves can employ. Following is a list of steps new principals can take to make their first year on the job a success.

1. Be clear about your mission. As a new principal, you need to clearly understand what your superiors expect of you during your first year. If such expectations are not outlined during selection or shortly thereafter, you should meet with your immediate supervisor to find out what you are expected to accomplish your first year on the job. Then, you should meet periodically with your supervisors to keep them informed of progress toward reaching agreed goals and expectations.

2. Seek information about district operating procedures. Developing a working knowledge of district operational procedures is vital to a new principal's ability to "get things done." Thus, if orientations to budgeting, curriculum, supervision and evaluation, decision-making processes, and other system-specific procedures are not scheduled, you should arrange to meet with personnel responsible for each area. In those meetings, you need to ask for specific details that will help you become familiar with written and unwritten procedures, expectations, timelines, and due dates required. Next, you need to mark these items on a calendar and develop a "tickler file" system to remind you of the administrative responsibilities you have in various areas. Finally, you should not hesitate to ask for further assistance throughout the first year. Trying to learn everything during the first month is unrealistic.

3. Prepare a list of questions for the outgoing principal. Each building in a school system has its own culture or way of doing things. Thus, you would be well advised to prepare a list of questions for the outgoing principal to gain clarification about building-specific operating procedures, schedules, staff strengths

71

and weaknesses, staff subgroup leaders, key community members, and so forth.

4. Find a veteran "buddy." If the district does not assign a veteran to assist a beginning principal, you should seek out a veteran who can provide you with technical information, assistance, and confidential guidance and support. The veteran will probably feel flattered by a new principal's desire to tap his or her wisdom and knowledge. And you should not only call that veteran periodically, but also ask the veteran to provide you with a sense of how well you are doing.

5. Be yourself. Although advice from a savvy veteran is valuable, you should avoid the temptation to imitate others' leadership styles and methods. You need to learn from others, but you also need develop an operating style that is natural and comfortable for you.

6. Get to know your staff. A leader's success is dependent on his or her ability to work with and through people to accomplish goals. Thus, it is imperative for you to get to know your staff members in order to develop relationships based on trust. Scheduling time to meet individually with each staff member is one useful way of encouraging dialogue and establishing trust. In those informal meetings, ask staff members what they like about the school and what they think needs to be changed. In addition, scheduling social events throughout the year can help you get to know staff members on a more informal basis. If out-of-school functions are held, invite everyone, but don't put pressure on people to attend.

7. Initiate change slowly. Before suggesting or initiating change, you need to develop an indepth understanding of the reasons underlying existing conditions. Involving staff members in assessing current norms and practices and inviting them to suggest changes are imperative to move a school through a successful change effort. Nevertheless, you should not avoid the responsibility of suggesting improvements and making final decisions.

8. Ask for feedback on performance. If you are unsure of superiors' perceptions of your performance, you should ask for specific feedback. Sharing your individual goals and actions with superiors is a good starting place for feedback discussions. Furthermore, at the beginning of the year you should ask how you will be evaluated, by whom, and how often. Finally, seek confidential feedback from staff members. Then, with feedback information in hand, develop specific objectives that will facilitate your growth.

9. Develop a support group. The demands of the principalship may be eased if you have individuals you can confide in and from whom you can seek emotional support. If you are married, a supportive spouse is vital; you and your spouse need to be aware that the first year will require long hours and mutual emotional support. Even so, you need to take time to play and relax with family, friends, and colleagues to balance your life at work and at home.

10. Maintain a sense of humor. The final area to check throughout the first year is your sense of humor. Beginning principals must be able to laugh at themselves and accept that they will make mistakes. Being able to laugh at yourself will, at the very least, help to create rapport between you and your staff.

Summary

Developing a capable cadre of men and women to serve as America's elementary and secondary school leaders is extremely important. The process starts with preservice training and continues through the phases of recruitment, selection, and induction. Training institutes, professional associations, school districts, and principals themselves must assume some responsibility for designing and carrying out a carefully planned developmental sequence. The payoff can be outstanding school leaders who clearly know their mission and who have the skills and necessary support to provide effective leadership.

The development of outstanding school leaders must not be abandoned, however, at the end of a principal's first year on the job. The following chapter addresses the issue of how school systems can sustain and enhance principals' performance after the first year.

PRINCIPALS

HOW TO TRAIN,
RECRUIT, SELECT,
INDUCT, AND
EVALUATE
LEADERS FOR
AMERICA'S
SCHOOLS

EVALUATING PRINCIPALS

Getting a top-notch principal does not end when the person is hired. Districts that commit time and resources to recruiting, selecting, and inducting capable principals face yet another challenge—evaluating them. Supervisory officials must develop and use sound strategies to ensure that principals continue to grow and develop effective leadership skills throughout their careers. A well-designed and comprehensive evaluation system is one way to better ensure such growth.

Current studies suggest, however, that the evaluation methods used by many districts are not designed to enhance principal performance, but to satisfy accountability requirements that make principal evaluation mandatory. In fact, many principals report that performance evaluations by superiors are infrequent or, if done at all, are not specific or helpful. Researchers Joseph Murphy, Philip Hallinger, and Kent Peterson (1985) contend that principal evaluation has remained "substantially unchanged." Many principals, they found, are "neither supervised nor evaluated on a regular basis."

As discouraging as this might sound, an encouraging sign documented in this chapter is that several educators and school districts are making efforts to improve methods of principal evaluation. After providing an overview of principal evaluation practices, this chapter focuses on three important phases of the evaluation process. Next, evaluation strategies that provide principals with specific, confidential feedback from superiors, peers, and teachers are highlighted, followed by a discussion of one district's exemplary principal evaluation system. The chapter concludes with recommendations for improving the methods school districts use to evaluate principals.

Current Practice in Principal Evaluation

On the heels of the school accountability movement that

flourished in the 1970s, public demand for administrator evaluation increased markedly in the U.S. during the 1980s. Because of a growing realization that principals are key players in influencing the performance and attitudes of students and faculty, formal evaluation procedures are now being advocated, researched, legislated, and implemented.

One indicator of this increased emphasis on assessing principals' performance is the growing number of states now mandating their evaluation. According to a 1988 report released by the Southern Educational Improvement Laboratory (Stephen Peters 1988), only two states required principal evaluation in the early 1970s, "but within a 10-year span from 1977 to the present, most states began or were planning to begin statewide programs for principal evaluation."

The Educational Research Service (ERS) (1985), which has been documenting administrative evaluation practices since 1962, found a similar increase in principal evaluation programs in its most recent nationwide survey of school districts. "The results of the 1984 ERS survey indicate that 85.9 percent of the responding districts currently have formal evaluation systems for administrators."

A dilemma that school districts and states face when evaluating principals is determining what purpose the process should serve—accountability, professional improvement, or both. After completing a study of principal evaluation practices in Oregon, Dan Duke and Richard Stiggens (1985) concluded that most school district evaluation systems appear to be designed for accountability; few "provide principals with the systematic feedback on performance they need to plan their professional development." Attempting to balance accountability and professional improvement is a tightrope school districts must walk in designing and implementing comprehensive principal evaluation programs.

Purposes of Principal Evaluation

Although the reasons for evaluating principals are numerous, they can be divided into two general categories:

1. *Formative Evaluation.* Evaluation serves as a means to help principals improve their performance. This evaluation process requires ongoing communication between superiors and principals, with the focus on improving

not only principal performance, but the overall educational program as well.

2. *Summative Evaluation.* Evaluation serves as an end, a judgment of performance on which to base principals' retention, promotion, demotion, incentive pay rewards, and other personnel actions.

Table 4, developed by ERS (1985), illustrates the differences between formative and summative evaluation and outlines the components of each approach.

Most districts responding to the ERS survey said they attempted to combine the formative and summative approaches; however, many principals contend the only feedback they receive

Table 4. Components of Two Major Purposes of Evaluation

Purpose of Evaluation	Role of Supervisor	Process	Uses	Focus
Formative Evaluation serves as a means to improve performance	Counselor	Ongoing communication, feedback, assistance	Improve performance; interrelated with decision-making, goal development, and other administrative tasks	The improvement of the educational system
Summative Evaluation serves as an end, a final judgment	Judge	Specific culminating judgment	Basis for merit pay, promotion, demotion, inservice training, transfer, and similar personnel decisions	The individual and his or her performance

Source: Educational Research Service (1985). Reprinted by permission.

is summative evaluation. William Harrison and Kent Peterson (1988) report that districts using only summative evaluation often fail to provide principals with the feedback necessary for professional growth and improvement. One principal in their study describes the inadequacy of such a practice: "Last year I was never visited by the evaluator and I received all 'superior performance' ratings—not very effective or helpful to me."

Districts that incorporate both approaches when evaluating principals accrue several benefits. On the summative side, school districts bolster their public image when they hold principals accountable for good work and dismiss or reassign incompetent principals. As Elio Zappulla (1983) states, "The public wants, and indeed deserves, some assurance from the board that the money it so agonizingly pays out in the form of property taxes, most of which goes toward employee salaries, is being used to pay the best people for doing the best job." Therefore, providing the public with evidence that a district rigorously evaluates principal performance is "not only advisable but indeed mandatory," according to Zappulla.

On the formative side, meaningful communication with and effective supervision of principals can not only enhance principals' performance but assist in improving the entire educational system. In a study of districts with effective principal evaluation programs, Murphy, Hallinger, and Peterson (1985) found that superintendents who used both formative and summative evaluation processes closely linked the yearly objectives of principals with board and superintendent goals. In addition, those superintendents utilized both processes to provide principals feedback, to build morale, and to model "what they believed were important aspects of school district management."

In the past few years, educators have developed a variety of models and procedures that combine the formative and summative processes into one comprehensive evaluation system. The next section outlines three important phases of principal evaluation that incorporate both processes.

Three Phases of Evaluation

To develop a systematic, successful evaluation program that satisfies the need for accountability and professional improvement, school districts must carefully plan and implement three phases:

1. *Planning for evaluation,* which involves analysis of a specific situation, establishment of purposes for evaluation, setting of goals and specific objectives, and deciding on means for measuring the processes used and the eventual outcomes.

2. *Collecting information,* which involves monitoring and measuring the activities planned and the outcomes that result from the activities.

3. *Using information,* which includes communication regarding the analysis and interpretation of information as well as making decisions about the next steps to be taken. (Dale Bolton 1980)

Bolton emphasizes that information analyzed in phase 3 provides the basis for reviewing principal performance and establishing new goals and objectives; "therefore, it becomes a natural prelude to the first phase, allowing the cycle to be repeated." This cyclical process is illustrated in figure 1.

Phase 1—Planning for Evaluation

As the first essential step toward planning an effective evaluation system, the school board, supervisory personnel, principals, and other district educators should specify the school system's values, philosophy toward evaluation, purposes of the process, and expectations of principals. Ronald Cammaert (1987) states that districts that develop "written statements of purpose which are clear, precise, and complete are more likely to produce a sound basis for open communication and cooperative relationships than programs designed around ambiguous or unwritten purposes."

Who Plans and How

A critical mistake made by many districts during this phase is failing to involve a broad base of school personnel in designing the evaluation system. According to Jerry Valentine (1987), change too often occurs from the top down. "A superintendent attends a conference or workshop, hears an exciting

Figure 1
A Three-Phase, Cyclical Process for Evaluation of Personnel

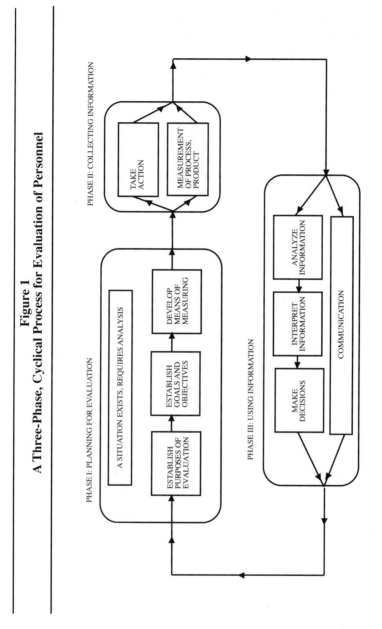

PHASE I: PLANNING FOR EVALUATION

PHASE II: COLLECTING INFORMATION

PHASE III: USING INFORMATION

A SITUATION EXISTS, REQUIRES ANALYSIS

ESTABLISH PURPOSES OF EVALUATION

ESTABLISH GOALS AND OBJECTIVES

DEVELOP MEANS OF MEASURING

TAKE ACTION

MEASUREMENT OF PROCESS, PRODUCT

ANALYZE INFORMATION

INTERPRET INFORMATION

MAKE DECISIONS

COMMUNICATION

Reprinted by permission of the publisher from Bolton, Dale L. *Evaluating Administrative Personnel in School Systems.* (New York: Teachers College Press, © 1980 by Teachers College, Columbia University. All rights reserved.) Page 40 - Figure 2.1.

speaker, returns to the homefront and mandates the change. This change process infrequently makes an impact." To ensure effective, enduring change in principal evaluation practices, Valentine recommends that a committee made up of principals, central office supervisory personnel, teachers, and board members should be responsible for planning the program.

Valentine also recommends using a consultant as a resource person during this phase. He cites a recent study of 405 districts implementing new evaluation systems:

> Those districts which used consultants implemented systems which were more effective, had more internal support, and were more likely to make a significant impact upon the educational program than districts which implemented new systems without the direct assistance of a consultant.

Clear Expectations Needed

Performance criteria—the determination and communication of performance expectations—appear to be the most critical aspect of the planning phase. William Harrison and Kent Peterson (1988) believe principals must "clearly understand their superiors' expectations" to perform successfully. Too many districts, however, fail to provide principals with a clear understanding of their expectations.

In their study of evaluation practices, Harrison and Peterson found many principals were uncertain about their superintendents' expectations. The authors contend that "superintendents must make their expectations for principal performance clear, ensuring that principals understand the tasks they are to accomplish, the criteria used to assess performance, the type of data used, and the ways performance outcomes are appraised." Duke and Stiggens (1985) found similar confusion among principals. It is vital, they conclude, that superiors do a better job of articulating their expectations for principal performance and "expend greater effort in explaining the evaluation system to those subject to it."

School districts that wish to clarify the performance expectations of their principals could begin by looking at published lists of skills or proficiencies of school leaders. For example, the National Association of Elementary School Principals (NAESP) has recently revised its *Proficiencies for Principals of Elementary and*

Middle Schools (1991). Based on the findings of school effectiveness research and the experience of administrators, NAESP's list of proficiencies translates knowledge about effective leadership behaviors into identifiable actions in the school. Although it would be unrealistic, the association acknowledges, to expect all principals to practice all the proficiencies, they provide targets that every principal should aim at.

A total of ten proficiencies are grouped under *leadership proficiencies* (leadership behavior, communication skills, and group processes); *supervisory proficiencies* (curriculum, instruction, performance, and evaluation); and *administration/management proficiencies* (organization management, fiscal management, and political management). Each proficiency is briefly defined and then elaborated in action terms. For example, the proficiency "communication skills" is defined as follows: "The image the principal projects forms the dominant perception of the school by students, staff, parents, and the community." To demonstrate this proficiency, the principal does such things as "uses active listening skills," "exemplifies the behavior expected of others," and "keeps communication flowing to and from the school."

In a school district that is instituting school-based management or some other kind of restructuring, the performance expectations of principals will likely shift to reflect the changed roles and responsibilities of both teachers and administrators. Skills in administration and management will remain important, but other skills and values may, at least in the transition period, receive greater attention in the district's appraisal system. In an Office of Educational Research and Improvement report on the implications of the restructuring movement for the changing roles of school leaders, Mojkowski (1991) recommends that districts and superintendents reward such aptitudes as flexibility, risk taking, courage, enablement, collaboration, and recognition.

Setting Goals and Objectives

Another important aspect of the planning phase is the development of district, building, and individual performance goals and objectives. A typical goal-setting program involves an annual organizational review during which district goals are set. Next, principals and supervisors establish specific goals and objectives on which principals will work throughout the year. Finally, principals, along with their staffs, set attainable school goals that represent desired outcomes for the year.

Valentine states that principals often set overly simplistic goals. From his research on the use of school goal setting for the purpose of assessing principal performance, Valentine found that goals set by principals frequently consisted of "statements about personal administrative skills rather than desired outcomes." Furthermore, he notes, "the goals frequently reflected activities already completed or nearly completed and did not make a significant difference in the quality of life or program of the school."

Valentine recommends that principals receive training in goal setting to help them identify meaningful school goals. In addition, he suggests that school faculties and principals limit the number of goals to four to six each year—"two or three unique to a particular school and two or three correlated with district goals." Once goals are established, principals can then set specific objectives that will help them and their staffs move toward desired outcomes.

A clear understanding of what is expected of principals, the development of districtwide and school building goals, and the identification of principal goals and objectives are prerequisites for engaging in activities in the second phase—collecting information.

Phase 2—Collecting Information: The Who, What, Where, When, and How of Evaluation

Collecting information or sampling performance is another important phase in the evaluation process. The data-collection phase, along with communicating results, is at the crux of the "formative" approach to evaluation. The formative phase of collecting information is the most important phase in an evaluation process designed to promote personal growth and organizational development. Valentine points out that at least "90% of the time and energy given to evaluative activities should be made in the formative phase."

Unfortunately, many principals report being unaware of what information is collected on their performance and how it is obtained. Only half of the principals surveyed by Harrison and Peterson "claimed to know how the superintendent accumulated information upon which they based their evaluations." It is important, therefore, that school officials not only develop and adopt sophisticated collection strategies, but also let principals know what, when, where, and how information will be collected and who will collect it.

Superintendent and Supervisors Collect Data

Superintendents or supervisors can collect data on principal performance by recording specific statements and actions made during onsite visits where they shadow the principal for extended periods. They can also observe principals in different settings such as at faculty meetings, parent conferences, teacher observation and evaluation conferences, and public meetings.

Valentine recommends that the evaluator schedule a preconference or at least make contact with the principal prior to "scheduled observations" to agree upon the "time and specific tasks to be observed." In addition, he suggests that evaluators make "unscheduled observations" to provide opportunities for observing more "typicality" in principal performance "than with the scheduled observation."

Although it appears that direct observation and supervision of principals by superiors are critical for obtaining reliable data, many superintendents and supervisors do not directly observe the performance of principals. In their study, Duke and Stiggens found that most evidence for principal evaluation derives only from superiors' perceptions of how principals perform rather than from direct observation. "One reason for why good evidence is missing may simply be the fact that supervisors of principals lack the time needed to conduct thorough observations," write Duke and Stiggens. Thus, one way to increase the likelihood that useful information will be gathered is to "involve other school personnel in collecting information on principal performance," they conclude.

Peer Collection Strategies

Peer observation and review is a promising new strategy for providing principals with feedback on their performance. One such information-gathering and feedback strategy is Peer-Assisted Leadership (PAL), featured in chapter 3. As Barnett notes, participating principals indicate that they benefit from shadowing and working with other principals and practice more self-reflection, a process found useful in helping them run their schools.

Peer supervision/evaluation is an innovation that has not yet achieved wide acceptance. Only 2 percent of districts in the 1985 ERS survey used peer supervision as part of their principal evaluation system. Duke and Stiggens, in their review of evaluation practices in Oregon, also found few systems using peer review as one component of evaluation. They surmised that the lack of interest in peer review may be a function of time constraints for principals or reflection of the competitive relationships among principals in the same district.

Client-Centered Feedback

Information and feedback from clients—teachers, parents, and students—can also be used to evaluate principal performance. However, as in the case of peer review, client-centered ratings of principal performance are not widely used. Fewer than 1 percent of the districts participating in the 1985 ERS survey reported that they systematically collect teacher, parent, or student perceptions of principal performance.

Through interviews with school leaders for *The Executive Educator*, Marilee Rist (1986) was able to document concern among school leaders about client-centered principal evaluation. Scott Thompson, former executive director of the National Association of Secondary School Principals, told Rist, "We have no objection to the informal, nonofficial evaluation of principals by teachers on a confidential basis. We do object, however, to the formal, official evaluation of principal by teachers with the evaluation filed in the principals' personnel records at the district headquarters." On the other hand, Donald Langlois (1986) contends, "no one is in a better position than teachers to determine whether a principal is performing satisfactorily." As we will see later in this chapter, teachers can provide principals with useful, specific performance feedback that they can use for improving their performance.

Other Data Collection Strategies

Artifacts can provide additional information about principal performance. Student test scores; written evidence of progress toward a principal's personal, school, and district goals; principal awards and recognitions; newspaper clippings, parent newsletters, and letters to staff and students; and logs of how principals spend their time are examples of artifacts that can be used in evaluation. Before the beginning of the school year, principals should be notified of the types of artifact data that will be required so arrangements can be made to collect those data. Supervisors should discuss artifacts with principals during conferences throughout the year as well as at the end of the year.

As we can see, a variety of school personnel can be involved in the collection phase of evaluation; however, it takes a great deal of time and effort to obtain useful, reliable information.

Phase 3—Using Information

Analyzing, interpreting, and making decisions based on the information gathered in phase 2 constitutes the last major phase of the evaluation. To use information effectively, it is vital that supervisors and principals discuss the information compiled throughout the year, not just summarize it in a report at year's end. As Bolton notes, "There is not much doubt that the process of communication is extremely important during Phase I. However, it becomes even more important during Phase III." Bolton suggests that there is often a tendency for the evaluator and the principal to avoid contact after data are collected. In addition, analysis, interpretation, and decision making often occur before the principal and evaluator confer with each other. When this practice occurs, writes Bolton, "the other person's insight is lost and poor decisions may be made."

Providing Feedback

Conferences between supervisors and principals are an important method of communicating feedback on performance. To be most effective, conferences must be carefully planned, purposeful, and held as soon after data collection as possible. As Bolton contends, "The accumulation of information over a long period of time is not as beneficial as providing it soon after events occur."

According to Valentine, effective conferences should be based on a principal's internal motivation to improve, not on external motivation from the evaluator. Thus, a skilled evaluator "promotes this internal motivation by involving the principal in the discussion and promoting self-assessment of skills through inquiry, probing questions, and comments." Effective conferences, therefore, are "more accurately described as a self-assessment, coaching conference than as a feedback conference," writes Valentine.

Interspersing constructive criticism and positive feedback throughout conferences is another strategy used by effective evaluators. From his research on principal evaluation practices, Valentine found that "evaluators [typically] spend the first thirty minutes of conferences discussing all the 'good' skills and save the 'bad' skills for the last few minutes." Such a practice promotes "inattentiveness during the 'strokes' due to anxiety while awaiting the 'zingers'." Thus, it is more effective to alternately communicate positive and negative feedback.

Making Decisions

Final summative reports should be written and decisions made about the next steps to be taken only after ongoing communication between the evaluator and principal has occurred throughout the school year. For the summative evaluation, the principal's performance and efforts throughout the year should be taken into account. Final judgments regarding performance should be based on each criterion (expectation) established during phase 1. In addition, during the summative evaluation conference, the evaluator should document the principal's progress toward school- and system-wide goals.

With summative information in hand, goals, objectives, and final growth plans should be developed, starting the cycle of evaluation over again, beginning with phase 1, planning for evaluation.

Decisions about Employment Status and Merit Pay

The final aspect of the evaluation process involves decisions regarding employment status and pay. Valentine argues that, regardless of when contractual decisions are made, such decisions should be based on data collected during the year and summarized in summative evaluation documents. "To determine employment on any basis other than the findings would be unfair to the principal," writes Valentine.

Merit pay or incentive pay is a special consideration in the evaluation process. According to its proponents, incentive pay enables districts to compensate principals according to their effectiveness, thus providing additional motivation for exemplary performance. When Duke and Stiggens asked principals to identify shortcomings in their current evaluation system, "more respondents cited lack of rewards for outstanding performance than any other problem."

Unfortunately, as the ERS reports, "experience indicates that developing an incentive pay system is a complicated process, and one that, even more than a standard evaluation system, requires careful planning and consideration." The following five components must be in place to increase the likelihood of successfully implementing a merit pay system for principals:

Component 1—A sound, districtwide decision-making process that encourages broad-based input from the whole staff.

Component 2—A salary schedule that accurately places administrative positions in a justifiable relationship to each other and reflects in financial terms the requirements and responsibilities of each administrative position.

Component 3—An assessment process that accurately defines the characteristics and activities of an excellent administrator and accurately discriminates between a superior and a below-average administrator.

Component 4—A conversion formula that financially rewards excellent administrative performance by converting assessment scores into salary increases.

Component 5—A review process designed to improve the assessment, salary, and merit system on a frequent basis. (Bruce Kienapfel 1984)

In view of the problems associated with implementing a sound merit pay system, districts might want to consider other ways of rewarding outstanding performance, such as incentives for professional development and opportunities for improvement. Later in this chapter, one district that uses such an approach as a part of its comprehensive principal evaluation system will be featured.

Whatever methods are used to evaluate principals, the hallmarks of an effective evaluation system include careful planning, a commitment to professional development as well as accountability, clear expectations and criteria by which principal performance is judged, collection of data from a variety of sources, and ongoing communication between evaluators and principals. Through a system that they trust and are confident in, principals must receive honest, constructive feedback. As we will see in the next section, providing principals with "confidential" feedback from superiors, peers, and teachers is a way to build trust and to help principals improve their performance.

Confidential Feedback Strategies

> People basically want to be competent and are interested in self-improvement. Yet, many evaluation systems are designed to find people incompetent. If you are genuinely interested in improving a person's performance, it can only be done when the person buys into it. There must, therefore, be a high trust level and a high degree of confidence in the process. (Gerald Bogen, College of Education, University of Oregon—Personal Interview, January 1989)

To take advantage of principals' desire to perform competently, educators are recognizing that a variety of people—not just central office supervisors—should be involved in providing principals with feedback. Because it is important to cultivate trust, the process must minimize the possibility that principals will suffer from a sense of losing face or self-respect. With this goal in mind, several educators and institutions have begun to develop confidential evaluation systems to help principals obtain useful feedback from superiors, peers, and subordinates.

The Excellent Principal Inventory

During the 1987-88 school year, the BellSouth Corporation, with assistance from the management development firm of Kielty, Goldsmith, and Boone of La Jolla, California, began development of the *Excellent Principal Inventory*, a unique evaluation instrument that enables principals to obtain confidential performance feedback from superiors, peers, and teachers. Kielty, Goldsmith, and

Boone has designed and implemented training and management evaluation programs for a number of large corporations including Weyerhaeuser, Boeing, Control Data, Cummins Engines, LaBatts, and BellSouth.

After BellSouth successfully used the performance feedback system with nearly 10,000 of its management personnel, the corporation sponsored the development of a performance feedback instrument and training session for principals in the nine southern states that BellSouth serves.

Organization Values and Commitments: The Starting Point

Bogen, an educational consultant with Kielty, Goldsmith, and Boone, notes that the first step in designing any performance feedback system is the identification of values and behaviors that are important to the organization and its members. Without first identifying an organization's key values, Bogen states, developing a list of performance criteria is meaningless. Thus, value statements describing attitudes and behaviors of excellent principals were identified during a series of sessions involving principals from across the country working together with personnel from Keilty, Goldsmith, and Boone. The following five key commitments, drawn from research on effective schools and literature on leadership and management, reflect the values and behaviors developed for the *Excellent Principal Inventory:*

OUR COMMITMENTS

To Student Success:

• Demonstrating Respect for Students

• Pursuing All-Around Excellence

To Teaching and Learning:

• Promoting Teaching and Learning

• Supporting Continuous Learning as a Lifetime Goal

To the School Staff:

• Demonstrating Respect for the School Staff

• Helping Individuals Improve

• Building a Collegial Staff

To Innovation:

• Supporting Creativity

• Supporting Upward Communication

To Leadership:

• Demonstrating Integrity

• Presenting Ideas

• Taking Responsibility

• Relating to External Constituencies

Indicators of Excellent Principal Leadership Behaviors

To reinforce the values and behaviors that constitute the Five Key Commitments of the "Excellent Principal," eighty-nine specific behaviors were identified for the inventory. The following items, under the "Commitment to Leadership" area, provide a sampling of performance indicators listed in the instrument.

COMMITMENT TO LEADERSHIP

Demonstrating Integrity

• Shows a high degree of personal integrity in dealing with others

• Does what he or she believes is right, although it may not be popular

• Lives up to personal commitments made to others

• Leads by example

• Strives to ensure that actions and words are consistent

• Demonstrates sensitivity and respect to those of different social and cultural backgrounds

Presenting Ideas

• Articulates a clear vision of the school's direction

• Makes sure that the school's objectives are clearly understood

- Communicates in an open and candid manner
- Presents ideas effectively when speaking
- Communicates effectively in writing
- Provides effective orientation for new assignments
- Avoids talking down to others

Taking Responsibility

- Takes responsibility and ownership for his or her decisions
- Encourages and accepts constructive criticism
- Admits to his or her mistakes
- Makes decisions in a timely manner
- Demonstrates self-confidence as a leader

Relating to External Constituencies

- Keeps parents and the community informed about the school and its program
- Encourages and listens to ideas from parents and community members
- Works with dissenting individuals or groups within the community to reach understanding
- Is willing to challenge the district office when appropriate
- Does not pass the buck or blame the district office or school board
- Is sensitive to the interests of different racial and cultural populations

Collecting Feedback on Performance

According to Bogen, principals distribute the feedback instrument to teachers in their schools as well as to peers and superiors who "they believe are knowledgeable about their performance, whose opinions they value, and individuals who they believe will provide honest feedback to help in their professional

Demonstrating Respect for the School Staff

	Classroom Teachers									Others								
	Number Responding	Highly Dissatisfied	Dissatisfied	Neither Satisfied nor Dissatisfied	Satisfied	Highly Satisfied	Your Average	company Average	Your Percentile	Number responding	Highly Dissatisfied	Dissatisfied	Neither Satisfied nor Dissatisfied	Satisfied	Highly Satisfied	Your Average	Company Average	Your Percentile
Date		1	2	3	4	5				Date	1	2	3	4	5			
27. Demonstrates respect and concern for people as individuals	15	-			-	-	15				8	-				1	7			
	8/88							5.0	4.3	100	8/88						4.9	4.7	60
28. Helps people feel their work is meaningful and important	15	-	-	-	-	-	15				8	-		-		2	6			
	8/88							5.0	4.4	100	8/88						4.8	4.7	50
29. Is more concerned with giving credit than taking it	15	-	-		-	-	15				8	-		-		1	7			
	8/88							5.0	4.3	100	8/88						4.9	4.5	80
30. Distributes instructional resources fairly and equitably	15	-		-	-	2	13				8	-		-		2	6			
	8/88							4.9	4.4	95	8/88						4.8	4.6	70
31. Avoids playing favorites	15	-	1	-	4	10					8	-	-	-		1	7			
	8/88							4.5	4.0	79	8/88						4.9	4.4	95
32. Gives staff members recognition for their outstanding achievements	15	-	-	-	1	14					8	-	-	-	2	6			
	8/88							4.9	4.5	90	8/88						4.8	4.6	65

Source: Kielty, Goldsmith, and Boone (1998)

development." In addition, participating principals complete the inventory to assess their own performance.

Guaranteeing anonymity is vital to the successful use of the *Excellent Principal Inventory*. Individuals are asked not to sign their names, but respondents indicate which one of three categories they fall into—teacher, other (peer and superior), or self.

Bogen emphasizes that this evaluation system is clearly separated from the summative evaluation process. "It is a personal and confidential evaluation process designed for professional growth, not as an accountability system for making decisions relative to promotion, demotion, rewards, transfer, or dismissal," he says. Thus, a consultant and the principal are the only ones who see and discuss the results; the results are not forwarded to supervisors.

After completing the *Excellent Principal Inventory*, respondents send it to Keilty, Goldsmith, and Boone's scoring service in Milford, Connecticut, which tabulates the scores and develops an individual performance profile.

Feedback Report

A crucial phase of the *Excellent Principal Inventory* program is providing principals with feedback about their performance and developing growth plans based on the results. The scoring service provides the principal with a detailed profile summary report that a trained consultant explains and interprets during an intensive feedback conference held during a two-and-a-half-day followup.

Feedback results are displayed in a series of tables and organized under the "Five Key Commitments" categories. The data for each category are further broken down into results for "Classroom Teachers" and "Others"—peers and superiors. In addition, an arrow indicates how principals rated themselves on each item.

A sample summary profile table is provided in figure 2. In this example, a principal receives high marks in the "Demonstrating Respect for the School Staff" category of the inventory's "Commitment to Staff" section.

Using the Feedback for Improvement

Principals and consultants spend time during the feedback conference discussing the results and developing strategies to improve areas of weakness. In addition, consultants use a summary report of all participating principals' scores to design specific training activities for principals to participate in during the two-and-a-half-day workshop sessions. Bogen reports that participating principals from the nine southern states involved in BellSouth's foundation efforts are excited about the program and see it as an excellent way of obtaining useful feedback.

Additional Confidential Feedback Instruments

Other educational practitioners and researchers are designing confidential feedback instruments similar to the Excellent Principal Inventory. In 1983, Jerry Valentine and Michael Bowman (1986) began development of the Audit for Principal Effectiveness using items generated from "an extensive review of the literature and research relative to the role of the principal." Valentine and Bowman validated the items with over 1,500 teachers and administrators from across the country. Revised and copyrighted in 1986, the feedback instrument now includes eighty performance items under the categories of "Organizational Development," "Organizational Environment," and "Educational Program."

West Chester Area School District in Pennsylvania (Langlois 1986) and Kalamazoo Public Schools in Michigan (Kienapfel 1984) are examples of school systems that have developed and used teacher and peer feedback programs for evaluating principals. Confidential feedback on principal performance from superiors, peers, and teachers appears to be a promising new formative evaluation strategy that school districts incorporate into a comprehensive evaluation system.

The next section describes how one district incorporates many of the necessary components into an efficiently designed and comprehensive principal evaluation program. This school system's evaluation program is a model that other districts might benefit from when developing and implementing their own principal evaluation systems.

Tigard School's Principal Evaluation Program

In 1986, Oregon's Tigard Public School District (1990-91 enrollment approximately 8,330 in 12 schools) began efforts to improve its principal evaluation program. Tigard's comprehensive evaluation system, entitled TAPE (Tigard Administrator Planning/Performance Evaluation), is a data/goal-based system related to student outcomes and performance standards. Using the effective schools research, TAPE emphasizes profiling and goal setting as keys to planning and documenting the results and effects of leadership.

The systematic way in which the district planned the new evaluation system has been crucial to its success. Superintendent Russell Joki states, "I think we did things right in that we went about developing it slowly and had broad participation at every level." In 1986-87, during the planning and design stages for TAPE, a team of central office administrators and building principals reviewed research on effective schools and administrative evaluation practices and visited other districts using new techniques for evaluating principals. TAPE was piloted in 1987-88 and implemented in 1988-89. "Now we have a system in place with which principals, the board, and supervisors are satisfied," says Joki. Nevertheless, the program is designed to be flexible and can change as "circumstances and expectations change and as the district receives new information and ideas," emphasizes Joki.

Purpose of the Evaluation System

The purpose of TAPE is to address the areas of accountability and professional development. The "P" in the acronym signifies that planning and performance are two important aspects of a comprehensive evaluation system. According to Joki, the Planning portion represents the "professional development component of evaluation" and the Performance part of the title characterizes "more of the accountability side." In addition to these two general purposes of evaluation, the district has identified several specific reasons for principal evaluation.

One key purpose of TAPE is to link principal evaluation with the district's desire to apply the results of research on effective schools. Tigard has devoted considerable time and energy to incorporating the research on effective schools into the design of district educational programs and practices. Project BEST (Building Effective Schools Together) represents "the district's efforts to use effective schools research," says Joki. Thus, BEST is a cornerstone of the district's new evaluation system for principals; the project emphasizes making decisions based on a variety of data, "rather than just making decisions from intuitive judgments," states Joki.

With data-based decision-making as an integral component of TAPE, the program has five specific purposes:

- To provide a structure for annual goal setting and self-appraisal
- To provide a structure for professional growth
- To provide a structure for supervisor evaluation
- To share BEST practices
- To provide a structure for board review and recognition of leadership performance

Performance Standards and Expectations

During development of the evaluation system, it was critical for Tigard to determine specific standards and behaviors that were valued by the district and to create a method of documenting principal performance and progress toward school and districtwide goals. After an extensive review of research on the characteristics of effective principals and considerable discussion among planning team members and principals, the district identified nine general review areas:

- General Administration
- Instruction
- Project BEST
- Student Programs
- Community Relations
- Coordinated Curriculum
- Staff Development
- Support Service Management
- School Budgeting

In each of the nine areas, the district planning team identified several specific performance standards denoting behaviors and values that support the general areas for which principals are responsible. These performance standards, according to the TAPE document, "are used as a guideline for goal setting, self-appraisal and performance review." The performance standards also represent principal job descriptions and district expectations for leadership. Following are examples of two of the nine general areas and the specific performance standards—behaviors and values—under each.

Area 2 - Instruction

Performance Standards:

- *Supervision.* Makes frequent supervisory visits and provides teachers/staff with specific and immediate feedback.

- *Teaching Strategies.* Promotes and demonstrates a variety of teaching strategies. A clear understanding of ITIP and related teaching models is evident.

- *Evaluation.* Demonstrates skillful use of clinical supervision during conferences and the writing of summative evaluations. All evaluation time lines are met; summative evaluations are completed before the last month of school. The supervision and evaluation of library, special education, counseling, involves (sic) appropriate support staff.

Area 4 - Student Programs

Performance Standards:

- *Student Oriented.* Demonstrates on a daily basis interest in and contact with students in a variety of settings.

- *Esteem Program.* Maintains student recognition and instructional student esteem (Positive Action) activities.

- *Discipline.* Keeps discipline rules centered on behaviors and corrective consequences. Considers circumstances in disciplinary actions.

- *Student Involvement.* Encourages student participation in school pride and decision-making via established pathways (leadership class, student government) for involvement.

100

Goal Setting and Planning

Goal-setting and planning are important components of TAPE. Each spring, the board of directors begins the process of planning and setting systemwide goals for the upcoming year. According to Joki, the board reviews various reports "that come to it through administrative groups and begins discussions about program and curriculum changes. With the advice from the superintendent, the board sets goals for the coming school year." The district goals then "become an important feature of TAPE and appear in everyone's TAPE document," says Joki.

At the same time, principals begin "looking at the coming year and organizing individual building goals for each area in TAPE," Joki points out. In the spring, principals submit a first draft of individual and school goals to the superintendent and schedule a conference for discussing their plans and incorporating districtwide goals. After input from the superintendent and other central office supervisors, principals submit a final plan by September 15 listing the approved goals in the "planning section" under each general review area. These goals then become a part of each principal's annual leadership plan. Once goals are identified, another important aspect of TAPE begins—the process of collecting data.

Collecting Data for Evaluation

Accumulating information about principal performance and progress toward targeted goals is an ongoing process in Tigard and one for which both principals and supervisors are responsible. According to one secondary principal, "One of the things the superintendent did in the planning of TAPE was to ask principals for feedback on the evaluation practices of central office administrators. Some of the input he got was that they needed to spend more time observing in the buildings" (Anderson 1989a). As a result, noted the principal, "a priority was set for central office supervisors to spend more time in the building, observing and working with principals."

A minimum of two formal supervisory observations per quarter (each year has three quarters) is required in each of the nine general review areas of the TAPE program. Supervisors often contact principals prior to a school-site visit and notify them of

Table 5. TAPE Supervisory School/Program Observation Form

SUPERVISOR _____   DATE _____

SCHOOL/PROGRAM OBSERVED _____

LEADERSHIP AREA(S) DISCUSSED: _____

[ ]   Area 1: Gen.
       Administration

[ ]   Area 2: Instruction or
       Supervision/Evaluation

[ ]   Area 3: Project BEST or
       Program Data Base

[ ]   Area 4: Student Programs

[ ]   Area 5: Community
       Relations

[ ]   Area 6: Coordinated
       Curriculums

[ ]   Area 7: Staff
       Development

[ ]   Area 8: Support Services
       Management

[ ]   Area 9: School/Program
       Budgeting

[ ]   Area 10: School/Program
       Budgeting

[ ]   Area 11: Mandated
       Program Compliance

[ ]   Area 12: _____

_ _

Comments: (Progress Noted or Target[s] Developed) _____

_____

_____

_____

_____

_____

_____

specific areas that will be observed. Unannounced observations are also held. According to Joki, "A principal may have half-a-dozen visits during a quarter, in addition to the two formal observations." Regardless of whether the visit is scheduled or unscheduled, supervisors discuss their observations with principals and complete a written report after each observation. A sample of the report form is provided in table 5.

Quarterly Review

At the end of each quarter, principals assess their performance and progress toward identified goals in each of the nine general review areas. Principals rate their performance as "P," indicating leadership performance is "progressing," or as "T," indicating leadership performance is "targeted" and needs improvement. According to Joki, "One of the unique characteristics of TAPE is the self-appraisal component. We want principals to be interested in reflective thought about their performance and about what is going on in their schools." Thus, the self-evaluation is an important part of the quarterly and summative review process.

In addition to principals' self-appraisal, supervisors also complete a quarterly report summarizing their observation data. If supervisors rate a performance area with a "T" (targeting leadership performance that needs to be increased), Joki says they must provide the principal with a written "statement explaining why the principal hasn't been progressing toward the performance standard and then work with the principal to develop a specific goal to meet the performance standard." Supervisors' and principals' ratings are then placed in the TAPE document under the quarterly review section of each general review area.

Staff Feedback on Principal Performance

Tigard also conducts an annual staff survey in each school using the Teacher Opinion Inventory. The survey, developed and copyrighted by the National Study of School Evaluation, not only seeks staff opinions on principal performance, but also gathers staff perceptions about the entire school program. According to Joki, each principal has a staff member administer and tabulate the survey responses. The information is used as a part of the principal's confidential self-appraisal. Listed is a sampling of questions in the opinionnaire that pertain to principal performance:

- What is your general feeling about the way you are treated by the principal?

    A. Very Satisfied
    B. Satisfied
    C. Neither satisfied nor dissatisfied
    D. Dissatisfied
    E. Very dissatisfied

- Do you think class visitations by your principal are supportive of your efforts to improve instruction?

    A. Always
    B. Most of the time
    C. About half the time
    D. Rarely
    E. Never

- When you have a disciplinary problem what help can you expect from the principal?

    A. All the help I need
    B. Most of the help I need
    C. About half the help I need
    D. Little of the help I need
    E. None of the help I need

Specific results of the survey are not shared with the central office; however, principals do share the general results with central office administrators.

As we can see, Tigard principals and their supervisors collect a variety of information throughout the year and communicate frequently about performance and progress toward goals. These efforts culminate in the final phase of the TAPE process—summative evaluation ratings and conferences.

Summative Review

While documenting the efforts made throughout the year on targeted goals and the various performance standards, principals and supervisors complete the summative rating section in each of TAPE's review areas. A conference called "the summative review" is scheduled. Although Joki delegates observation and evaluation responsibilities to assistant superintendents, he is very involved in the evaluation process. "I believe the superintendent should be involved on some level of contact for supervisory purposes with principals," says Joki. Thus, he meets with each assistant who observes a principal and reviews the information so that "when I sit down with principals I have my own observations and also input from other assistants."

The following descriptors are used by principals and supervisors to indicate level of performance in each of the nine review areas.

E —*Exemplary*. An Exemplary rating indicates that the performance is regarded as a major success, or BEST practice. As a BEST practice, and Exemplary rating could serve as a model for other administrators. Exemplary ratings may be accompanied by Profile documentation and a BEST practice outline.

C —*Competent*. A Competent rating indicates that the performance is regarded as meeting the general expectations of the district. A Competent rating indicates that the performance is regarded as above average.

A—*Acceptable*. An Acceptable rating indicates that the performance is regarded as average and a potential growth target. An Acceptable rating, therefore, may be accompanied with improvement goal(s).

U —*Unacceptable*. An Unacceptable rating can only be given by the supervisor. An Unacceptable rating indicates that the performance is regarded as sub-standard or below average. An Unacceptable rating must be accompanied with an explanation and improvement goal(s).

NA—*Not Applicable*. A Not Applicable rating indicates that the administrator's assignment does not substantially include the area responsibility. A Not Applicable rating must have the supervisor's agreement.

During summative review conferences, principals and supervisors review the data collected during the year along with the self-appraisal and supervisory ratings. They also set goals and begin planning for the following year, starting the TAPE cycle over again.

Describing perceptions of the entire process, one elementary principal told me, "I am very positive about the TAPE process and feel about it the way I would hope my teachers feel about the process when it comes time for formal evaluations. It is an accumulation of all the things that represent your very best efforts."

Exemplary Performance Incentive

The TAPE program offers rewards for exemplary performance. Although the rewards do not include merit pay, Joki says, they do "provide incentive for outstanding performance." Principals who receive exemplary performance ratings in one or more areas of TAPE are eligible for a professional growth incentive, but the superintendent ultimately decides which principals will receive the exemplary performance reward. Selected principals choose one of four possible options:

1. Attendance at a national convention.

2. A personalized professional investigation in an area of interest. For example, a principal may want to spend a week learning about a related field such as medicine or journalism.

3. Memberships in other professional organizations.

4. Open. A plan may be worked out between the principal and the superintendent.

Principals can also obtain the professional growth incentive through self-nomination or peer nomination. "There are times and things that happen during the course of the year," says Joki, "that are significant and stand by themselves, apart from TAPE." Thus, principals can be nominated for the exemplary performance reward in the following areas:

Crisis Management: Exemplary performance during an unexpected or extraordinary event. In this category, the principal "manages" the material and emotional stages of the event by providing stability, anticipating and responding to the event's complexity, and focusing staff, community, and students on the positive and the future. As a result, there is community support, staff "togetherness" and student well-being.

Outside Recognition: Selection by a prominent agency or group for exemplary leadership. In this category, the principal is recognized for professional achievement that promotes school, program, or district goals. As a result, the professional image of the principal and the district is greatly enhanced.

Innovation: Successful implementation of an approved pilot program. In this category, the principal provides leadership that adapts or develops a program that produces significant student or staff achievement. As a result, student or staff competence and/or esteem is increased.

Research: Completion of major research that contributes to or promotes increased efficiency and/or effectiveness of students or staff. In this category, the principal researches and may publish a theoretical study that advances the profession and/or goals of the district. As a result, new ideas are generated for discussion and possible implementation.

Cost Savings: Leadership that produces significant cost savings without sacrificing efficiency or effectiveness. In this category, the principal designs and implements an idea or program that greatly reduces program cost while maintaining or increasing program success. As a result, the program and/or district uses its resources with greater returns at less cost.

A Distinguished Performance Review Committee consisting of one elementary principal, one secondary principal, a central office administrator, two retired administrators, and the superintendent confidentially review all nominations and determine those principals who will receive the Distinguished Principal Recognition. Selected principals are then recognized at the administrative council and school board meetings.

As we have seen, the TAPE evaluation program provides a comprehensive framework for assessing and enhancing principal performance. Planning, collection of objective data, clear expectations for principal performance, incentives for exemplary performance, and ongoing communication with and close supervision of principals are hallmarks of the system. When asked what advice he would give to other districts interested in improving their evaluation process, Joki recommends proceeding slowly, involving a broad base of people in designing the system, and developing a document that is "goal based and flexible."

This chapter demonstrates that principal evaluation must be thoroughly planned and carefully implemented to ensure professional competence and growth among school leaders. What remains is to summarize some of the key findings in the form of recommendations to districts that want to improve their principal evaluation process.

Recommendations for Evaluation

1. Identify the purposes of evaluation. First, school officials and other members of the district must identify the district's philosophy concerning evaluation and the purposes of the process. Although the reasons for evaluating principals may be numerous, districts should commit themselves to encouraging professional growth (formative purpose) and ensuring district patrons that principals are competent (summative purpose).

If the evaluation system is to be effective, the purposes must be discussed, identified, and agreed upon by everyone involved in the process. Developing a succinct written statement of philosophy that articulates the purposes of evaluation and summarizes the values of those affected by the process is, therefore, advisable.

2. Develop clear performance expectations. Once the purposes of evaluation are identified, school districts should identify the attitudes and behaviors that district members value in principals. Those values should be translated into a clearly written set of performance standards and expectations that will serve as the basis for judging principal performance. Then, superintendents must communicate those expectations to principals and ensure that principals understand the criteria that will be used to assess their performance.

3. Involve principals in planning. To develop an evaluation process that will be embraced by principals, districts must involve them in the development of the program. Forming a committee comprised of principals and central office personnel appears to increase principal understanding and support for evaluation programs.

Planning or revising evaluation methods should be done carefully, slowly, and systematically. To better ensure that a sound system will be designed and implemented, districts may want to consult other districts that have effective evaluation systems, review research on effective leadership and exemplary evaluation techniques, and perhaps even contact a knowledgeable consultant.

4. Encourage goal setting and self-reflection. Districts are advised to encourage, or even require, principals to set individual and school goals that will enhance their performance and contribute to systemwide goals and objectives. For these principals' goals to be effective, the board and superintendent must first set meaningful and timely goals for the district so that principals can incorporate those when they formulate their own goals. Principals may need assistance in developing goals that will have a significant impact on the school program.

Districts should also encourage principals to spend time reflecting on their performance. Self-appraisal of performance and progress toward written goals is an activity that principals engage in throughout the year. The familiar adage "You don't have to be ill to get better" characterizes the importance of principals' analyzing areas for improvement and developing a specific plan to enhance their performance and professional growth.

5. Observe principals in action and often. It is clear that evaluation and supervision of principals are improved when superintendents or central office supervisors devote ample time to working with and observing principals. Superintendents or supervisors should schedule periodic school visitations throughout the year for the purpose of observing principal performance. Preconferences should occur prior to visits to identify the reasons for an observation and specific activities to be observed.

Using scheduled and unscheduled observations, supervisors should carefully record principals' words and behaviors for analysis and interpretation during postobservation conferences. Conferences between supervisors and principals should occur as soon as possible after observations in order to analyze, interpret, and discuss collected data. During those conferences, constructive feedback should be interspersed with positive feedback. Evaluators should then assist principals in developing a plan for growth that includes specific learning objectives and needed resources.

6. Involve peers and teachers in providing feedback. Although principals' supervisors should assume the primary responsibility for observations and evaluations, districts should also consider soliciting confidential feedback from peers and teachers.

A collegial supervisory model, such as *Peer-Assisted Leadership*, can provide principals with useful feedback on their performance.

In addition to a principal's peers, teachers are also in a good position to determine whether a principal is performing satisfactorily. Thus, using an instrument such as the *Excellent Principal Inventory* to collect teachers' perceptions is another promising strategy for enhancing principals' self-appraisal efforts. For this strategy to be effective, teachers must be guaranteed anonymity and the principal should not be required to share the results with central office supervisors. Also, principals should receive assistance interpreting the results of teacher feedback. Therefore, it may be prudent to use a confidential consultant to help principals develop productive strategies for improving areas of weakness.

7. Collect artifacts. Principals and their supervisors should collect other information that provides evidence of the effects of leadership. Student test data and evidence of curriculum and instructional efforts; written evidence of principals' progress toward individual, school, and systemwide goals; newspaper clippings and letters to students, parents, and teachers; and logs of how principals spend their time are examples of artifacts that may be used. For the data to be effective, principals and supervisors should decide early in the year the types of data to be collected and the way it will be used.

8. Adopt a cyclical approach to evaluation. Evaluation should be a continuous process. Three important phases—planning, collecting, and using information—should guide the design process. Attention must be given to each phase, but particular emphasis should be placed on collecting and communicating information throughout the year. Districts that concentrate solely on the summative phase do little to improve principal performance. From the careful planning for evaluation conducted in phase 1 and the rigorous collection and sharing of information in phase 2, use of the information in phase 3 should naturally lead to another three-phase cycle of evaluation. Such a systematic process is necessary in order for supervisors to make meaningful decisions about employment status and pay.

9. Reward outstanding performance. Districts should reward those who exercise outstanding school leadership. Public recognition, letters of appreciation, and professional growth opportunities are ways superiors can recognize those principals who excel. Because cash incentive programs are difficult to design and administer, professional development opportunities may be a more promising method of rewarding those principals whose performance is exemplary.   The responsibility and motivation for professional improvement, however, should not rest solely with supervisors. Principals must be committed to improving their skills. Growth ceases without commitment to continued improvement. Evaluation systems, therefore, should be designed so that evaluation is a mutual effort between principals and their superiors. Such cooperative efforts are necessary to ensure that America's schools will be led by capable principals.

CONCLUSION

All of the principals in the United States, assembled
together, would just fill the Rose Bowl. This is an
unlikely assemblage, to be sure, but one that illustrates
the importance of principals who can define and promote
educational excellence. (U.S. Department of Education
1987)

The role of the principal is probably one of the most influential
positions affecting school effectiveness. The familiar adage "so
goes the principal, so goes the school" accurately characterizes the
importance of a principal's leadership. Although better preparation, selection, induction, and evaluation of school leaders will not
provide a total solution to educational problems, it offers an
important beginning.

An effective preparation process based on a clear view of
the principal's role, combined with better recruitment, selection,
induction, and evaluation techniques, can help revitalize American schools. As the U.S. Department of Education's Principal
Selection Guide states, the preparation, selection, orientation, and
development of school leaders "is one of the most economical
options for significantly improving schools."

School districts, therefore, cannot afford to leave the identification, preparation, and selection of principals to chance. Instead, school systems and universities must be committed in both
policy and action, ensuring an adequate pool of capable, trained
candidates. Next, school systems must use sound selection methods to pick the best. Getting a "cracker-jack" principal does not
end, however, with selection. School districts must also develop a
comprehensive set of induction procedures for orienting and
supporting newly hired principals. Finally, school districts need
to design and use a comprehensive evaluation system that provides principals with timely, useful performance feedback that
enhances their professional growth. If they do not, even the best
principals will never achieve their full potential.

Effective school reform does not occur as a result of state mandates or edicts from the nation's capitols. It happens school by school, initiated and guided by capable principals. Thus, developing, selecting, and supporting school leaders is key to providing American school children with an excellent education.

BIBLIOGRAPHY

$\mathbf{M}$any of the items in this bibliography are indexed in ERIC's monthly catalog *Resources in Education (RIE)*. Reports in *RIE* are indicated by an "ED" number. Journal articles that are indexed in ERIC's companion catalog, *Current Index to Journals in Education*, are indicated by an "EJ" number.

Most items with an ED number are available from the ERIC Document Reproduction Service (EDRS), 7420 Fullerton Rd, Suite 110, Springfield, VA 22153-2852.

To order from EDRS, specify the ED number, type of reproduction desired—microfiche (MF) or paper copy (PC), and number of copies. Add postage to the cost of all orders and include check or money order payable to EDRS. For credit card orders, call 1-800-443-3742.

Anderson, Mark E. *Evaluating Principals: Strategies to Assess and Enhance Their Performance: OSSC Bulletin Series.* Eugene: Oregon School Study Council, University of Oregon, April 1989a. 53 pages. ED 306 672.

_____. "Helping Beginning Principals Succeed." *OSSC Report* 30,2 (Winter 1990): 1-7. (Oregon School Study Council, University of Oregon).

_____. *"Hiring Capable Principals: How School Districts Recruit, Groom, and Select the Best Candidates.* OSSC Bulletin Series. Eugene: Oregon School Study Council, University of Oregon, May 1988a. 40 pages. ED 297 436.

_____. *Inducting Principals: How School Districts Help Beginners Succeed.* OSSC Bulletin Series. Eugene: Oregon School Study Council, University of Oregon, October 1988b. 60 pages. ED 304 764.

_____. *Inducting Principals: A Study of the Job-Specific Information and Assistance Needs of Beginning Principals in Oregon and Washington.* (Doctoral Dissertation, University of Oregon, 1989b.) *Dissertation Abstracts International,* 50, 3421A.

_____. "Training and Selecting School Leaders." In *School Leadership: Handbook for Excellence*, 2nd ed., edited by Stuart C. Smith and Philip K. Piele. 53-84. Eugene, Oregon: ERIC Clearinghouse on Educational Management, College of Education, University of Oregon, 1989c. ED 309 507

Association of Washington School Principals. "New Principals off and Running." *The Principal in Olympia*. Bulletin no. 1 (Fall 1988): 1.

Baltzell, Catherine D., and Robert A. Dentler. *Selecting American School Principals: A Sourcebook for Educators*. Cambridge, Massachusetts: Abt Associates, Inc., January 1983. 68 pages. ED 236 811.

Barnett, Bruce G. "Peer-Assisted Leadership: Using Research to Improve Practice." *Urban Review* 17,1 (1985): 47-64. EJ 324 749.

Barnett, Bruce G., and Faye L. Mueller. "The Long-Term Effects of Inservice Training for Principals." Paper presented at the annual conference of the American Educational Research Association, Washington D.C., April 1987. 23 pages.

Barth, Roland S. *Run School Run*. Cambridge, Massachusetts: University Press, 1980.

Bass, Bernard M. "Leadership Training and Management Development." Chapter 33 in *Stogdill's Handbook of Leadership*, edited by Bernard M. Bass. New York: The Free Press, 1981.

Bolton, Dale L. *Evaluating Administrative Personnel in School Systems*. New York: Teachers College Press, 1980.

Boyer, Ernest L. *High School: A Report on Secondary Education in America*. Carnegie Foundation for the Advancement of Teaching. New York: Harper and Row, 1983. 380 pages. ED 242 227.

Bridges, Edwin M. "The Nature of Leadership." In *Educational Administration*, edited by L. L. Cunningham, W.G. Hack, and R. O. Nystrand, 202-230. Berkeley, California: McCutchan Publishing, 1977.

Cammaert, Ronald A. *A Study of the Current Practices for the Evaluation and Supervision of Principals in Alberta*. (Doctoral Dissertation, University of Oregon, 1987.)

Clark, Vivian K. "The Effectiveness of Case Studies in Training Principals, Using the Deliberative Orientation." *Peabody Journal of Education* 63,1 (Fall 1986): 187-95. EJ 354 956.

Cline, Dwight D., and Mike D. Richardson, "The Reform of School Administrators Preparation: The Kentucky Principal's Internship Model." Paper presented at the annual convention of the National Council of Professors of Educational Administration,

Kalamazoo, Michigan, August 1988. 27 pages. EA 021 595.

Cornett, Lynn M. *The Preparation and Selection of School Principals.* Atlanta, Georgia: Southern Regional Education Board, 1983. 20 pages. ED 231 052.

Daresh, John C. "The Beginning Principalship: Preservice and Inservice Implications." Paper presented at the annual meeting of the American Educational Research Association, Washington D.C., April 1987a. 18 pages. ED 280 196.

_____. "The Highest Hurdles for the First Year Principal." Paper presented at the annual meeting of the American Educational Research Association, Washington, D.C., April 1987b. 27 pages. ED 280 136.

_____. "Principals Perceptions of Collegial Support as a Component of Administrative Inservice." Paper presented at the annual meeting of the Mid-Western Educational Research Association, Chicago, Illinois, October 1982. ED 275 048.

_____. "Questioning the Assumptions of Field-Based Preparation Programs." Paper presented at the annual meeting of the Mid-Western Educational Research Association, Chicago, Illinois, October 1987c. 17 pages.

Department of Elementary School Principals. *The Elementary School Principalship in 1968.* Washington D.C.: National Education Association, 1968. 28 pages.

DuBose, Elizabeth. *A Study of the Task-specific Assistance and Information Needs of Incoming Elementary School Principals in South Carolina.* (Doctoral dissertation. University of South Carolina, 1986.)

Duke, Daniel L. *School Leadership and Instructional Improvement.* New York: Random House, 1987.

Duke, Daniel L., and Richard J. Stiggens. "Evaluating the Performance of Principals: A Descriptive Study." *Educational Administration Quarterly* 21,4 (Fall 1985): 71-98. EJ 329 615.

Educational Research Service. *Evaluating Administrative Performance,* Arlington, Virginia: ERS, 1985. 144 pages.

Erlandson, David A., and Gonzalez, Y. "Principals Experience Growth and Renewal." *The School Administrator,* (February 1988).

Fliegner, Laura R. "'Action Interviews' Show You Who Can Cut the Mustard." *The Executive Educator* 9,4 (April 1987): 17-18. EJ 349 210.

Goodlad, John I. *A Place Called School: Prospects for the Future.* New York: McGraw-Hill, 1983.

Hagler, Thomas E.; Martha J. Jones; and Kenneth M. Matthews. "Field-Based Preparation of Leadership Personnel." Paper presented at the annual meeting of the University Council for Educational Administration, Charlottesville, Virginia, October 1987. 12 pages. ED 228 260.

Harrison, William C. and Kent D. Peterson. "Evaluation of Principals: The Process Can Be Improved." *NASSP Bulletin* 72,508 (May 1988): 1-4. EJ 371 965.

Hughes, Everett. *Men and Their Work.* New York: Free Press, 1958.

Janis, S.L. *Victims of Groupthink.* Boston, Massachusetts: Houghton-Mifflin, 1972.

Jensen, Mary Cihak. *Recruiting and Selecting the Most Capable Teachers.* OSSC Bulletin Series. Eugene: Oregon School Study Council, University of Oregon, May 1986. 22 pages. ED 269 885.

Kentucky Association of School Administrators and Appalachia Educational Laboratory. *A Statewide Program of Support for Beginning Administrators: The Kentucky Institute for Beginning Principals.* Charleston, WV: Appalachia Educational Laboratory, November 1987. ED 296 454.

Kielty, Goldsmith, and Boone. *The Excellent Principal Inventory.* La Jolla, California: Kieltly, Goldsmith, and Boone, 1988.

Kienapfel, Bruce. "Personnel Policies for Administrators." In *Merit Pay for Administrators: A Procedural Guide.* 40-42. Arlington, Virginia: Educational Research Services, 1984. ED 248 601.

Langlois, Donald E. "The Sky Won't Fall if Teachers Evaluate Principal Performance." *The Executive Educator* 8,3 (March 1986): 19-20.

LaPlant, James. *Principals Inservice Program.* Dayton, Ohio: Institute for Development of Educational Activities, August 1979. 21 pages. ED 186 993.

Lee, Ginny V. "Reaching Broader Audiences: Training Trainers to Deliver Peer-Assisted Leadership." Paper presented at annual meeting of the American Educational Research Association, New Orleans, Louisiana, April 1988. 33 pages.

Licata, Joseph W., and Chad D. Ellett. "Toward a Clinical Induction System for School Principals." Paper presented at the annual meeting of the University Council for Educational Administration, Cincinnati, Ohio, October 1988. ED 301 938.

Lindsay, James W. "Groom Your Assistants for the Big Time." *The Executive Educator* 7,2 (February 1985): 41,48. EJ 313 654.

London, M. *Developing Managers.* San Francisco, CA: Jossey-Bass Publications, 1985.

Lortie, Dan. *School Teacher.* Chicago: University of Chicago Press, 1975.

Louis, Meryl Reis. "Surprise and Sense Making: What Newcomers Experience in Entering Unfamiliar Organizational Settings. *Administrative Science Quarterly* 25, (1980): 226-251.

Manasse, Lorri A. *Improving Conditions for Principal Effectiveness: Policy Implications of Research on Effective Principals.* Washington, D.C.: Dingle Associates Inc., June 1983. 50 pages. ED 245 355.

Marrion, Barbara A. *A Naturalistic Study of the Experiences of First-Year Elementary School Principals.* (Doctoral Dissertation, University of Colorado at Boulder, 1983.) *Dissertation Abstracts International,* 44, 939A.

McCormick, Kathleen. "The Vaunted School Executive Shortage: How Serious Is It?" *The Executive Educator* 9,6 (June 1987): 18-21. EJ 353 921.

McDermott, Donald F. "A Long-Range Approach to Instructional Leadership." *Educational Leadership* 41,5 (February 1984): 64 pages. EJ 293 152.

Mojkowski, Charles. *Developing Leaders for Restructuring Schools: New Habits of Mind and Heart.* A report of the National LEADership Network Study Group on Restructuring Schools. Washington, DC: Office of Educational Research and Improvement, U.S. Department of Education, March 1991. 72 pages.

Murphy, Joseph; Philip Hallinger; and Kent D. Peterson. "Supervising and Evaluating Principals: Lessons from Effective Districts." *Educational Leadership* 43,2 (October 1985): 78-82. EJ 327 943.

National Association of Elementary School Principals. *Principals for 21st Century Schools.* Alexandria, Virginia: NAESP, 1990. 55 pages.

_____. *Proficiencies for Principals of Elementary and Middle Schools.* Revised edition. Alexandria, Virginia: NAESP, 1991. 58 pages.

National Association of Secondary School Principals. *Performance-Based Preparation of Principals: A Framework for Improvement.* Reston, Virginia: NASSP, 1985. 38 pages. ED 257 211.

_____. "Improving the Selection of Principals: An Analysis of the Approaches." *NASSP Bulletin* 72,508 (May 1988): 35-38. EJ 371 971.

National Commission for the Principalship. *Principals for Our Changing Schools: Preparation and Certification.* Fairfax, Virginia: National Commission for the Principalship, 1990. 50 pages.

National Policy Board for Educational Administration. *Improving the Preparation of School Administrators: An Agenda for Reform.* Charlottesville, Virginia: NPBEA, May 1989. 33 pages. ED 310 493.

National Study of School Evaluation. *Teacher Opinion Inventory.* Falls Church, Virginia: National Study of School Evaluation, 1981. 7 pages.

Nelson, Robert A. *The Organizational Socialization of Public School Administrators.* (Doctoral Dissertation, University of Oregon, 1986.) *Dissertation Abstracts International,* 47, 3928A.

Northwest Regional Educational Laboratory. *Questions and Answers about Leadership for Excellence. What Is It? Is It for You?* Portland, Oregon: NWREL, September 1988. 11 pages.

Peters, Stephen. *State-Mandated Principal Evaluation: A Report on Current Practice.* Southern Educational Improvement Laboratory, July 1988. 75 pages. ED 292 889.

Peterson, Kent D. "Obstacles to Learning from Experience and Principal Training." *Urban Review* 17, 3 (1985): 189-200. EJ 329 073.

Pharis, William L. and Sally Banks Zakariya. *The Elementary School Principalship in 1978: A Research Study.* Arlington, Virginia: National Association of Elementary School Principals, 1979.

Rist, Marilee C. "Principals Mull the Merits of New Evaluation Techniques." *The Executive Educator* 8,4 (April 1986): 36- 38. EJ 334 265.

Rogus, Joseph F. and William R. Drury. "The Administrative Induction Program: Building on Experience." *NASSP Bulletin* 72,508 (May 1988): 11-16. EJ 371 971.

Schainker, Stanley A., and LaRaine M. Roberts. "Helping Principals Overcome On-The-Job Obstacles to Learning." *Educational Leadership* 45,1 (September 1987): 30-33.

Schmitt, Neal, and others. "The NASSP Assessment Center: A Validity Report." *NASSP Bulletin* 66,455 (September 1982): 134-42. EJ 268 244. Schmuck, Richard. "Beyond Academics in the Preparation of Educational Leaders." *OSSC Report* 28,3 (Spring 1988): 1-11. (Oregon School Study Council, University of Oregon.)

Schmuck, Richard. "Beyond Academics in the Preparation of Educational Leaders." *OSSC Report* 28,3 (Spring 1988): 1-11. (Oregon School Study Council, University of Oregon.)

Smith, Mary Wilbert. "David Douglas Recruits and Trains New Administrators from Its Teacher Corps." *OSSC Report* 27,3 (Spring 1987): 10-12. (Oregon School Study Council, University of Oregon.)

Sosne, Howard L. "Advice to Rookies: Dos and Dont's for Making That First Year Successful." *Principal* 62,1 (September 1982): 14- 17.

Tigard Public Schools. "Planning/Performance Review Administrator Evaluation" (TAPE document). Tigard, Oregon: Tigard Public Schools, 1988. 14 pages.

University Council for Educational Administration. *Leaders for America's Schools: The Report of the National Commission on Excellence in Education.* Tempe, Arizona: UCEA, 1987. 65 pages. ED 286 265.

U.S. Department of Education. *Principal Selection Guide.* Washington D.C.: Office of Educational Research and Improvement, U.S. Department of Education, June 1987. 43 pages. ED 282 358.

Valentine, Jerry W. "Performance/Outcome Based Principal Evaluation." Paper presented at the annual convention of the American Association of School Administrators, New Orleans, February 1987. 24 pages. ED 281 317.

Valentine, Jerry W. and Michael L. Bowman. *Audit of Principal Effectiveness: A User's Technical Manual.* Columbia, Missouri: Valentine and Bowman Publishers, 1986. ED 281 319.

Wasden, F.D., I. Muse, and G.F. Ovard. "Preparing Principals in a School-University Partnership." *Principal* 67,1 (September 1987): 16-18. EJ 358 006.

Webster, E.C. *The Employment Interview: A Social Judgement Process.* Schomberg, Ontario, Canada: S.I.P. Publications, 1982.

Weldy, G.R. *Principals: What They Do and Who They Are.* Reston, Virginia: National Association of Secondary School Principals, 1979.

Zakariya, Sally Banks. "How to Add Snap, Crackle, and Pop to Principal Selection." *The Executive Educator* 5,11 (November 1983): 20-23. EJ 288 173.

Zappulla, Elio. *Evaluating Administrative Performance: Current Trends and Techniques.* Belmont, California: Star Publishing Company, 1983.

INTERVIEWS

Gerald Bogen, Associate Dean, Division of Educational Policy and Management, College of Education, University of Oregon, Eugene, OR. Interview January 4, 1989.

Karen Fearing, Administrative Assistant, Institute for Development of Educational Activities, Inc., Dayton, Ohio. Telephone Interview July 26, 1988.

Russell (Russ) Joki, Superintendent, Tigard School District 23J, Tigard, OR. Interview January 6, 1989.

Ginny Lee, Peer-Assisted Leadership Trainer, Far West Laboratory, San Francisco, California. Telephone Interview July 20, 1988.

Anthony (Tony) Palermini, Superintendent, David Douglas School District 40, Portland, OR. Interview February 9, 1988.

Barbara Rommel, Staff Development Coordinator, David Douglas School District 40, Portland, OR. Interview February 9, 1988.

Ron Russell, Assistant Superintendent of Personnel, David Douglas School District 40, Portland, OR. Interview February 9, 1988.

OTHER PUBLICATIONS

The Collaborative School: A Work Environment for Effective Instruction

Stuart C. Smith and James J. Scott • Foreword by Roland S. Barth • 1990 • xii+77 pages • perfect bind • ISBN 0-86552-092-5 • $8.00. (Copublished with National Association of Secondary School Principals.)

What are *collaborative schools*? In contrast to many schools where the adults work in isolation from one another, teachers and administrators in collaborative schools work as a team. Through such practices as mutual help, exchange of ideas, joint planning, and participation in decisions, the faculty and administrators improve their own skills and the effectiveness of their schools.

This book outlines the educational benefits of collaboration, describes a variety of collaborative practices already in use in schools, and suggests ideas for introducing those practices in other schools that wish to become more collaborative.

Roland S. Barth says in the foreword: "There is good news in the message of this book: Collaboration is being increasingly recognized as not only a desirable but an essential characteristic of an effective school; many schools have made huge strides toward shared leadership and collaboration; and the principal can be a central force in making a school a more collaborative living space."

Managing the Incompetent Teacher, *Second Edition*

Edwin M. Bridges with the assistance of Barry Groves • Second Edition • 1990 • 84 pages • saddle bind • ISBN 0-86552-102-6 • $6.95.

Here is an up-to-date revision of the Clearinghouse's best-selling book. Professor Bridges added significant new information in such areas as teacher evaluation criteria, use of student test scores, evaluation of teachers by parents, remediation procedures, and grounds for dismissal. In addition, the final chapter, "Putting Theory into Practice," has been rewritten in its entirety.

Bridges presents an integrated organizational approach in which teacher dismissal becomes a logical extension of overall school policy. "Superintendents who follow this systematic approach should be able to upgrade the quality of their teaching staff, to increase the incidence of dismissal when teachers fail to improve, and to heighten the prospects of winning a dismissal case if it is contested by the teacher."

Restructuring Schools: Educators Adapt to a Changing World

David T. Conley • February 1991 • 49 pages • saddle bind • 0-86552-110-7 • $7.00.

After defining restructuring, this paper describes restructuring efforts in 11 dimensions: curriculum, instruction, measurement/ assessment, time, technology, learning environment, school-community relationships, governance, working relationships, personnel, and teacher leadership.

The economic, social/political, and technological forces driving the school restructuring movement are also described.

School Leadership: Handbook for Excellence

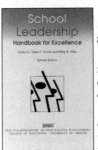

Edited by Stuart C. Smith and Philip K. Piele • Second Edition • 1989 • xvi + 392 pages • perfect (sew/wrap) bind • ISBN 0-86552-096-8 • $15.95.

This handbook suggests the knowledge, structure, and skills necessary for a leader to inspire all members of the school community to work together toward the goal of an excellent education for every student.

Rather than summarizing research findings as an end in itself, each chapter includes one or more sections that spell out implications, recommendations, or guidelines for putting knowledge into practice. The book is also, as Edwin M. Bridges says in the foreword, "highly readable."

Fifteen chapters are grouped into three parts:

Part 1. The Person
- Chapter 1. Portrait of a Leader
- Chapter 2. Leadership Styles
- Chapter 3. Training and Selecting School Leaders
- Chapter 4. Two Special Cases: Women and Blacks

Part 2. The Structure
- Chapter 5. School-Based Management
- Chapter 6. Team Management
- Chapter 7. Participative Decision-Making
- Chapter 8. School Climate

Part 3. The Skills
- Chapter 9. Leading the Instructional Program
- Chapter 10. Leading the Instructional Staff
- Chapter 11. Communicating
- Chapter 12. Building Coalitions
- Chapter 13. Leading Meetings
- Chapter 14. Managing Time and Stress
- Chapter 15. Managing Conflict

Professor Bridges states, "For school leaders or aspiring leaders . . . I am confident that this book will become a valued resource, one to which they will turn and return as they confront the timely and timeless issues which this book addresses."

Voices from the Classroom: Educational Practice *Can* Inform Policy

David J. Flinders • Foreword by Milbrey Wallin McLaughlin • 1989 • x+82 pages • Saddle bind • ISBN 0-86552-093-3 • $7.75.

Discussions about educational policy too frequently exclude the teacher's voice. Consequently, many policy directives and administrative decisions fail to take into account the realities of teachers' work.

In an effort to restore the teacher's perspective, David J. Flinders presents case studies of three high school English teachers. Then he devotes three additional chapters to outlining the major "lessons" and policy implications of this research.

As Milbrey McLaughlin, associate professor of education at Stanford University, states in the foreword, "Flinders allows us to experience the everydayness of teaching, the frustrations, the rewards, and the adaptations that inevitably result when teachers try to reconcile their values, goals, and energies with the classroom realities they confront."

Working Together: The Collaborative Style of Bargaining

Stuart C. Smith, Diana Ball, and Demetri Liontos • Foreword by Charles Taylor Kerchner • 1990 • xii + 75 pages • saddle bind • ISBN 0-86552-103-4 • $6.75.

In some school districts, teacher unions and district officials are exchanging an adversarial style of labor relations for a more cooperative process that emphasizes problem-solving, mutual respect, and team involvement in the education process. This book's descriptions of collaborative bargaining practices being tried by various school districts, along with practical guidelines and pitfalls to avoid, make the volume a good starting-point for educators interested in adopting a more collaborative process.

The authors offer twenty-four guidelines to consider before, during, and after collaborative bargaining. Emphasis is on building trust, enhancing communication and negotiation skills, and developing workable procedures.

The Appendix allows four key national organizations to present position statements on the new methods of bargaining and make comments about this book. The statements were solicited from the American Association of School Administrators, the American Federation of Teachers, the National Education Association, and the National School Boards Association.

Collaboration with Social Service Agencies

Professionals in both the education and the social service systems now recognize more clearly than ever the need for a team effort. Problems such as poverty, drug abuse, sexual abuse, street crime, homelessness, teenage pregnancy, dropping out of school, and sexually transmitted diseases are too big and too complex for either the schools or human service agencies to tackle alone.

Recently, the ERIC Clearinghouse on Educational Management teamed up with Oregon's Linn-Benton Education Service District to launch a multivolume handbook series that gives school personnel a practical guide for collaborating with social service agencies in their own communities.

Four of six planned volumes in the series, titled *At-Risk Youth in Crisis: A Handbook for Collaboration Between Schools and Social Services*, are now in print.

Volume 1: Introduction and Resources provides essential background information. It describes the Handbook's rationale, its benefits, how it was developed, and how educators can adapt the Handbook to their own communities.

It also contains resources on collaboration between schools and social services. These include two *ERIC Digests* and a set of resumés of journal articles and research reports that were identified in a search of the ERIC database.

Subsequent volumes deal with specific crisis issues: suicide, child abuse, substance abuse, teen parents, school attendance, and so forth. Each volume suggests guidelines for school staff to follow as they respond to immediate crisis situations. In addition, each volume presents long-term prevention strategies, staff and student training programs, policy development guidelines, and other practical materials.

For example, *Volume 2: Suicide* includes nine chapters dealing with such elements as facts about suicide (prevalence, motives, and myths), warning signs, key helping skills, steps for responding to suicidal youth with an emphasis on team decision-making, suicide prevention training, steps for developing policies and procedures, legal requirements, and examples of school suicide prevention programs.

Thus the Handbook serves as a model for both content (substantive guidelines for responding to particular crisis situations) and process (procedures helpful to schools and social service agencies when entering into collaborative relationships).

At-Risk Youth in Crisis: A Handbook for Collaboration
Between Schools and Social Services

Volume 1: *Introduction and Resources*
(February 1991) 58 pages
ISBN 0-86552-108-5

Volume 2: *Suicide*
(March 1991) 74 pages
ISBN 0-86552-109-3

Volume 3: *Child Abuse*
(May 1991) 54 pages
ISBN 0-86552-111-5

Volume 4: *Substance Abuse*
(June 1991) 53 pages
ISBN 0-86552-112-3

Coming in 1992:
Volume 5: *School Attendance* and
Volume 6: *Teen Parenting*

All Volumes are 8.5 X 11 inches,
saddle bind

Price:
$7.50 per Volume;
set of Volumes 1-4, $24.00.

Value Searches

Value Searches are economical, user friendly collections of ERIC resumés on the following high-demand topics:

- Parent Involvement in the Educational Process
- Instructional Leadership
- School Choice, Vouchers, and Open Enrollment
- Leadership of Effective Schools
- Collegiality, Participative Decision-Making, and the Collaborative School
- Professional Development of Teachers and Administrators
- Teacher Recruitment and Selection
- At-Risk Youth and Dropout Prevention
- Recruitment and Selection of Superintendents and Principals

Purged of irrelevant citations, Value Searches consist of bibliographic information and abstracts from ERIC's two reference catalogs: *Resources in Education (RIE)* and *Current Index to Journals in Education (CIJE)*.

For each Value Search, the index terms used in the search and the time period covered are listed in an introduction. Instructions for using the search materials and ordering copies of the complete documents and journal articles are included.

The resumés are printed on a laser printer in an easy-to-read large type, and they are durably bound.

Whereas an original ERIC database search would cost a minimum of $30.00, Value Searches are priced at only $7.50 each. Value Searches are updated several times each year so that they include the latest materials.

A Leader's Guide to Mentor Training

Edited by Judith Warren Little and Linda Nelson • February 1990 • 323 pages • 3-hole punched • ISBN 0-86552-099-2 • $20.00 ($25.00 with View Binder Notebook). (Copublished by the Far West Laboratory for Educational Research and Development and the ERIC Clearinghouse on Educational Management.)

This comprehensive guide was created by staff developers in the Los Angeles Unified School District. The thirty-hour training program is organized into seven modules: preparing mentors for work with beginning teachers; orientation to the mentor role; assisting new teachers; classroom organization and management for new teachers; classroom consultation, observation, and coaching; mentor as staff developer—presentations and inservice training; and cooperation between the administrator and the mentor.

Full payment or purchase order must accompany all orders. A handling charge ($2.50 domestic, $3.50 international) is added to all billed orders. Make checks payable to **University of Oregon/ERIC.** Address orders to ERIC/CEM, 1787 Agate Street, Eugene, OR 97403. (503) 346-5044. FAX: (503) 346-5890. Expect 6-8 weeks for delivery. (To expedite delivery, you may specify UPS for an extra charge.)

Returns: If materials are returned in saleable condition within one month from the date of shipment, we will refund 90% of purchase price; within six months 70%; within one year 50%. **The following quantity discounts apply to orders of each title:** 10-24 copies 15%, 25-49 copies 20%, 50+ copies 25%.